The
Compassionate
Visitor

The Compassionate Visitor

Resources for Ministering to People Who Are Ill

Arthur H. Becker

AUGSBURG Publishing House • Minneapolis

THE COMPASSIONATE VISITOR
Resources for Ministering to People Who Are Ill

Library of Congress Cataloging in Publication Data

Becker, Arthur H.
    THE COMPASSIONATE VISITOR

    Bibliography: p.
    1. Church work with the sick.   I. Title.
BV4335.B38   1985   259'.4   84-28370
ISBN 0-8066-2094-3 (pbk.)

Manufactured in the U.S.A.   APH 10-1620

1   2   3   4   5   6   7   8   9   0   1   2   3   4   5   6   7   8   9

Contents

Acknowledgments

In preparing this volume I am indebted to my students at Trinity Lutheran Seminary who over many years have shared with me their experience in care of the sick. In sharing verbatim accounts of their visits, they have often bared their souls, exposing their own fumbling, fears, and anguish, even as they endeavored to enter compassionately into the world of suffering of the sick persons they were visiting. To name all these students whose detailed accounts of their visits have enhanced this volume would exceed the bounds of confidentiality. They all have enriched my understanding of the art of ministry, even as I hope their understanding and sensitivity has grown in our dialog.

All of us are also indebted to the many sick persons who have shared their anguish with me in my pastoral ministry and with the students who were their friends and comforters. As always in true ministry, the one who would seek to comfort and to give also becomes the receiver and the comforted. In many ways the sick person ministers even while being the recipient of ministry.

To members of my own family who have shared their experience, have taught me sensitivity and compassion, and have allowed me in some ways to minister to them and who have blessed and supported my ministry, I wish also to express my gratitude.

And certainly, also, much of the credit for this book goes to Mae Wagner, who faithfully and without weariness typed and retyped drafts of the manuscript. To my daughter Carol Becker Smith, who edited and re-edited, goes a great deal of the credit for whatever readability this volume has.

Ministry is never a solo affair. This is as true in a seminary context as it is in a parish. As the minister in the congregation is surrounded with a great cloud of living witnesses, so are we in a seminary. Not only students are our teachers, but colleagues as well. To my esteemed colleagues at Trinity, who have been my teachers and ministers, I wish to express my gratitude. It is to them that I dedicate this volume.

Preface

It has been a long-standing conviction and fond hope of mine that care and compassion for the sick become not only a most important part of the ministry of the pastor but a primary ministry of the entire congregation. Ministry to the sick is, after all, a ministry of the whole congregation, which is sometimes delegated to the ordained pastor or other ministers. This explains the consistent use of the word *pastoral* in the book written for lay persons who take up this ministry of compassion.

In writing this book I have thought of three levels of care for the sick and suffering. The first involves us all as human beings; care and compassion for the sufferer is one of the hallmarks of being a human being. We could label it *Christian* caring, since we are called in Baptism to be merciful as our heavenly Father is merciful.

The word *pastoral*, for the purpose of this book, and in the thinking of many in the church, does not refer exclusively to ordained clergy, but to that work done by anyone in the body of Christ on behalf of the congregation. Anyone who carries out a ministry of comfort and of Word and prayer as a representative of the body of Christ is performing pastoral functions. Thus the person who serves as lector is serving as a pastoral person, or *assisting minister*, according to *Lutheran Book of Worship*. This is then the second level of compassionate caring, carried out by anyone as a delegated representative of the congregation.

The third level of caring, fulfilled by the ordained pastor, is a presiding ministry centered in Word and sacrament again, as delegated representative both of the congregation and of the Lord Jesus himself. A basic assumption of this book is that lay visitors will be sent out by the congregation to their ministry and will be presided over by the ordained pastor.

It is my hope that this book may enhance the ministry of the church in the care for the sick. May it bring even greater comfort and solace to those for whom we are compassionate friends.

1

The Experience of Illness

Nothing in life is so precious to us as health. Our self-image is deeply tied to it. When health is threatened by pain or illness, *we* are threatened. It is as if the very core of our being were under attack. For this reason, we deeply need and profoundly long for support, comfort, and assurance in any illness. For this reason we also almost instinctively reach out with compassion to someone who is ill—even as we shrink from too close contact, lest we be captured by the illness of the other. For this reason pastoral care is critical at the time of illness. So throughout the history of the church, visiting the sick has been a high priority of the ministry of the congregation—and of the pastor.

Health is also profoundly related to our spiritual life—to our salvation. It is fortunate that contemporary understanding of health no longer is limited to physical well-being, or, more narrowly, to the absence of disease entities, but includes spiritual, psychological, and physiological well-being or wholeness. Under the label of wholistic health (also spelled "holistic"), a new movement is springing up that endeavors to understand the implications of health and healing from this broader perspective and to promote its acceptance. For centuries people have known or sensed that the health of the body, or the person, involved more than what modern medicine calls "disease." In African tribal and ancient biblical consciousness, for example, two large categories of illness are perceived: one (involving injury or trauma) an *external* assault on the integrity of the body; the other, *internal,* an assault on the very person, the being of the individual. In the latter case, the question always is, *Who* causes the illness? This is in contrast to much of Western technical medicine where the question is *what* caused the illness. Our concern should be both *what,* as well as *who,* "causes" illness. Our understanding of this *who* will be different from the primitive conceptions which involve being bewitched by an enemy or a deceased family member whom one had not properly honored in death. As foreign as these conceptions may be, they point to an important truth: underlying illness in some way are broken, conflicted relationships with one's family, one's neighbors, or with God. This is an insight that we who are concerned for pastoral care should cherish. This awareness that personal relationships clouded by conflict, fear, hate, or guilt have as much to do with being sick as bacteria, viruses, or trauma is as important for pastoral care as for modern medicine. It is from this vantage point that we will explore the resources and procedures for pastoral care in illness.

What does it mean to be sick?

If we are to make intelligent and fully helpful visits to the sick, it is important to understand how illness affects the person. Illness isolates, but other effects are equally important to understand. It will be very helpful if the visitor can remember an experience of illness of his or her own—perhaps what it was like to be a hospital patient for the first time.

I suspect that everyone who has been in a modern hospital has experienced the feeling of entering an alien world which was supposed to help, but was so filled with mystery and anonymity that it was uncomfortable. There is a great need for warm, friendly human contact. It is this, above all, that the "sick call" should provide. If it fails in this, it adds to the distress of illness rather than providing relief.

Wayne Oatcs has identified the following character-istics of the experience of illness and hospitalization.

Illness disrupts the routine of living

The patient is *separated* from familiar surroundings. For almost any adult this means separation from the routine of work, which often is one of the major foun-dations of self-esteem, the source of a sense of worth and meaning for life. The sick person frequently feels as though he or she were "lying down on the job," figur-atively as well as literally. This fosters a sense of guilt that one is not supporting the family as one should, and a feeling of "deserving" the punishment of illness.

For most of us, our work routine also is the way we keep at bay our gnawing anxieties about the meaning of life, the prospect of failure or success, our fear of death, anxiety about our worth to others, and whether we are loved or not. A sick person often muses, "You sure have a lot to think about, lying here looking at the ceiling all day." These fundamental anxieties of life are most often what sick people think about.

Being separated from the family is another significant aspect of illness. We assume that sick children will miss their parents and be homesick, but we mistakenly assume that adults are grown-up and no longer have these feelings of loneliness and homesickness. The longing to be at home is a welcome sign that the family relationships are meaningful.

Another aspect of being separated from the family is the disruption of normal life and activity. This is rarely mentioned to the minister in the course of pastoral visiting, but the visitor should be sensitive to it, so that if there is a need, it can be discussed without embarrassment or surprise. A significant way in which this disruption may express itself is in straining the marriage relationship. The apostle Paul was sensitive to this (1 Cor. 7:3-6). An ill person may wonder what his or her spouse is doing—with whom he or she is associating—and may offer expressions of jealousy and even hostility. The visitor should be sensitive to these expressions as possible symptoms and should not too quickly brush them aside.

For older people the issue of the sexual life of the marriage often finds expression in concern about the continuance of sexual activity following an illness, or the effect of the illness on such activity. This is particularly notable in cases of heart conditions and the recuperative program following heart attacks. Often the patient is reluctant to speak of this either to the physician, pastor, or spouse, and with tact the lay visitor can be helpful in encouraging or even helping the patient to open up channels of communication.

Illness is costly

Illness is also costly from a financial perspective. Though many patients have health insurance or Medicaid, this impact is felt in two ways: first, in the earning capacity of the patient, and secondly, in the cost of the illness itself. Though direct medical costs may be covered, daily income ceases, and this can be a matter of considerable worry to the patient.

A closely related anxiety is the patient's sense of competence, especially if he or she is the chief breadwinner of the family. There may be the fear of letting down the family, of being a shirker, or even being a personal failure. One of the central components of self-esteem for each of us is our work or our profession, and when this is stripped away by a sudden crisis or illness, the shock to our whole way of thinking about ourselves is profound. This cannot be overcome by simple reassurance, or, worse yet, brushed aside by comments such as, "Don't worry about your job. Right now you've got all you can do to think about your health." If what we have said earlier about the all-inclusive nature of health and illness is true, then "illness" in the area of one's job or self-esteem, is as significant as "sickness" of the heart or gall bladder. Indeed, worries about one's adequacy or competency can be as insidious as cancer.

The continuing escalation of health costs generates anxiety about the larger costs of illness—several hundreds of dollars a day for hospital care, specialized procedures, and physicians. A patient may well begin to wonder whether it is all worth it. In our culture we are valued—and we value ourselves—for what we can produce. But this attitude comes home to roost when money is being spent *on us* instead! We would like to tell the sick person, "Look how valuable you are to us. We are spending thousands of dollars a day to make you well." But if the patient already feels guilty and a failure, he or she is likely to feel the reverse—"I'm not worth all the money you are spending!"

There is also an ethical dimension here that we have not yet come to terms with as a society or as a church. A patient may well feel that a disproportionate amount of family and societal resources are being spent on just one person—or to buy just one more month, week, or day of life. By profligate spending for medical care we may be saddling the sick person with a tremendous sense of obligation. The patient may feel, "It cost society and my family $40,000 to keep me alive. Now I'd better pay it back, or else prove that I was worth it!" Concerns of this sort must be heard by the visitor and resolved between the patient and family. Often the biblical teaching of the unmerited grace of God can be helpful here.

Illness: a family affair

The feeling of loneliness, the fear of adding to the burden of the family by one's illness, the anxiety about what the costs of care are doing to family resources all indicate very clearly that illness is a family affair. The visitor should keep this constantly in mind and do everything possible to keep open and strengthen avenues of love and care between family members and the individual who is ill. It is easy to overlook this important responsibility, because the need of the sick person seems so overwhelming in contrast to the needs of other members of the family; even the family tends to concentrate all its energies on concern for the one who is sick, sometimes to the detriment of the total life of the family or the individual needs of family members. This situation is most marked in the case of children; if one child is ill, particularly with a chronic or terminal disease, often attention is so centered on the sick child that other siblings either are—or at least feel—neglected. This is one reason for the often unexpected marital breakdown as an after-math of serious illness in the family. It is as if the structures of the family were subjected to loads heavier than they could bear, and they were shattered by the burden of illness.

Illness "infantilizes"

Illness also tends to "infantilize" the patient. Anyone who goes into a hospital experiences this almost immediately. It begins to happen when a nurse or hospital attendant commands ("requests" is a kinder word, but the patient knows they are commands): "Please take off all your clothes and put this on." So the patient must wear what looks like a shroud and feels like a tent, a gown with no buttons and with the flaps (always to the rear!) open to the wind. All the patient's personal belongings, those little things that provide a sense of being an individual, are taken away and he or she is put to bed, almost like a child. From that moment on the infantilization of the patient continues. He is told when to eat, what to eat, when to sleep, and when to go to the potty. Sometimes he is even fed like an infant, and the potty is provided. He feels like a one-year-old, totally dependent on mother. The nurse becomes mommy; the doctor becomes the distant all-powerful father whom one dares not cross; other patients become siblings—maybe brothers and sisters in misery; ward aides, practical nurses, technicians, and other staff members become the older siblings who care for their little brothers and sisters. Even though most of this is necessary in order to provide the kind of care the patient needs, it often has a destructive effect.

In order to be healed of any illness, a patient has to learn dependency and trust. For some this is exceedingly difficult. The typical "self-made man" rebels vigorously at being forced to be so utterly dependent. Suddenly one who is used to making decisions and managing the affairs of an organization or business must now take orders and depend on others. For one to whom this responsibility has been a core of self-understanding, the threat is profound. Suddenly the great American ideal, the self-made man or woman, is no longer an asset but a liability. While in the past this threat particularly affected men, the feminist movement has increased its impact on women as well.

Often the only way the patient can react to this is by hostility, which has to be directed toward the wrong persons. The patient dare not be angry at the nurse, because "she is only trying to help." And no one would dare be angry at the doctor! After all, "You don't bite the hand that heals you!" So the anger has to be directed at others who won't or can't fight back; and it finds itself expressed in griping about the hospital food or complaining that the nursing staff (especially aides) are inattentive: "I ring the bell a hundred times before they answer!" Often the anger gets directed toward members of the family for their supposed inattentiveness and lack of concern. It is helpful if the visitor can remember this and carefully interpret what seems to be totally uncalled-for hostility. And finally, anger may be directed toward God and toward the minister or hospital visitor. Once again, it is important to understand what such anger may be indicating and that it should not be taken personally. This is not the time to undertake a defense of the hospital, the nurses, the physicians, the family, or God; it is the time to understand why the patient is angry.

The regressive impact of illness throws the patient back on the most basic of human attitudes, trust—trust in those who are providing care. This does not come automatically; it has to be learned. It is learned in infancy as one implicitly trusts parents and other caretakers, and is rewarded by their loving care. Ideally, the care on which one depends does not make one a *helpless* dependent, constantly at the mercy of the decisions of caretakers; rather, it generates trust in which one grows toward increasing autonomy and individuality, without feeling that one is deserting or even betraying those who are giving the care. Good parenting, good medical care, and the care God gives not only allow but encourage participation and growth, cooperative interaction between the one cared for and the one who gives care.

Here the dynamic of religious faith becomes significant. If the patient trusts God as a compassionate parent who is interested in and invites one's personal growth, who does not provide all the answers but does provide all the resources for dealing with life and its problems, that faith will be a valuable resource in the battle against illness and suffering. If, on the other hand, the patient trusts that God will provide all the answers and make all the decisions, the patient will neither have the resources nor the will to engage in the struggle against disease, or even to cooperate effectively with the physicians and all others who are intervening on behalf of health and life.

Illness isolates

A person who is ill and in pain feels lonely and isolated. Patients often feel that no one understands their pain, worry, and fears. They may fear that "no one else can do anything about it," and this often culminates in the despairing wish: "Let me suffer alone."

Pain and suffering have an isolating effect because, in marshalling all personal resources to face and attack the suffering, the sufferer becomes necessarily self-centered; there just isn't enough emotional or physical energy left to think about anything or anyone else. A further form of self-isolation then takes place which is reinforced by the reaction of family members and others to the "self-ishness" of the patient (if that self-centeredness is not understood).

A further cause of isolation in illness is the feeling that the patient is to blame or that illness is a prime indicator of wickedness. These feelings cause the patient to feel undeserving of the attention and care of others. Though no member of the family may consciously acknowledge it, there are often deep feelings of this sort on the part of members of the family and the larger community regarding illness. This may be especially true in cases of illness due to accidents or failure to excercise good judgment.

Harbinger of death

Every illness, no matter how minor, is a reminder of our mortality. Even the shortest hospitalization poses a threat to our sense of self-sufficiency and our dream that somehow death comes only to other people. Our pervasive denial of death in this culture (see Ernest Becker's book *The Denial of Death*) makes it difficult for the patient to express fear of death without being scorned or scolded. The minister or representative of the community of faith who openly acknowledges death is one of the few persons with whom the patient can confess this fear. And it is significant how often this theme is raised, albeit in various disguises that the perceptive listener can recognize.

Rarely will a patient say outright, "I'm afraid I'm going to die." To use the word "die" or "death" about oneself is almost taboo. The pastoral visitor must, therefore, be very careful how he or she responds to these subtle references. But one must always hear them, and the first time they are verbalized one must often simply file them away for future reference when the relationship is stronger.

The experience that most sharply arouses our fear of dying is surgery. Often it is not surgery itself, no matter how serious, that generates this fear. It is the anesthesia. Except for the coma of cardiac arrest, drowning, or other similar phenomena, the absolute "sleep" of anesthesia is as close as we can come to death itself. Anesthesia is like a "little death." This is why good surgical teams in modern hospitals will schedule a consultation by the anesthesiologist, usually the day before surgery, to explain the procedure and to quiet the fears of the patient. This is also why it is important to visit *before surgery* if at all possible. The dread of "going under," as patients sometimes put it, is one of the reasons that even minor illnesses remind us of our mortality.

These fears should never be taken lightly or be responded to with superficial or premature reassurance—nor, on the other hand, should they be taken so seriously that a morbid and defeatist attitude is stimulated in the patient. Here again, the simple, warm, compassionate, steady acceptance on the part of the visitor is most helpful—one that neither condones nor condemns these dark and hidden fears that plague us all. Here again, the solid reliance on the simple faith that we are always in God's hands is the most helpful. This is one of the basic messages that the pastoral visitor should be prepared to bring.

Why visit the sick?

We visit the sick out of a concern for the restoration of physical and spiritual wholeness. But beyond that, what is the specific agenda? It is important that we come to terms with this basic question if our visits are to be effective and satisfying, both for us and for those we visit.

The most important reason for "making sick calls," as my pastor father used to describe them, is because they have for centuries been a traditional part of the church's life. This was in immediate response to the example of Jesus himself, whose mission to proclaim the kingdom of God was characterized by his healing ministry. The biblical understanding of God as the "God of steadfast love and mercy" who was personalized in Jesus is demonstrated most vividly in his compassion for the troubled in spirit (Mark 1:23) and for those who were ill (Mark 1:32). It is this same sense of compassion for suffering and hurting people that motivated the early church to care for the sick (James 5:13-15). Compassionate caring seemed to the early disciples to be most consistent with the name of Jesus Christ of Nazareth (Acts 3:1-6). And so it seems to us today. Visiting the sick is and should be one of the highest priorities for the pastoral care program of the congregation.

While usually carried out by the pastor, there is ample biblical and historical evidence that this ministry has been carried out by other representatives of the community of faith (James 5:13-16; Acts 3:1-6). Therefore any member of a congregation who wishes to engage in this ministry should consider the possibility of doing so.

The first reason we visit the sick, then, is to follow the example of Christ—and the tradition of the church, which has continued to follow his example through the centuries.

We may well ask why Christ, and later the church, regard this as such a vital task. One of the central characteristics of God which the ancient Hebrews recognized was God's compassionate mercy. Throughout the biblical record, the theme continues. God does not forget us in our sufferings, whatever form they may take. God is with us in them. To the persecuted congregation of the dispersion came words of encouragement in their suffering. "Though now for a little while" they had to "suffer various trials," the writer reminded them of the bond between themselves and the Lord. He voiced his hope that the fiery trials would refine their faith, "that the genuineness of your faith, more precious than gold which though perishable is tested by fire, may rebound to praise and glory and honor at the revelation of Jesus Christ" (1 Peter 1:3-10; see also Romans 5:2-10).

A further reason for visiting the sick is to break through the defensive walls of self-isolation. Isolation has to be invaded from the outside if the bonds of personal and spiritual relationships are to be sustained and strengthened and if hope and courage are to be nurtured. As God always reaches out to us in our isolation, so we are to reach out, in God's name, to those who feel deserted. In this breakthrough into the island of suffering there is healing. It is difficult to calculate the effect of just having someone be there when we are sick or in pain. And if that person is a symbolic person who represents the whole family of faith, or the human family, or the larger community, the healing effect is compounded.

Another reason for visiting the sick is to sustain and enhance the will to live, the courage to fight illness, the willingness to cooperate in the battle against illness. In recent research the importance of the patient's attitude toward illness and recovery has received renewed emphasis. This awareness has been lacking in the past and is due in no small measure to the tendency of medical practitioners and others (such as pastors and chaplains) who care for the sick to feel they have a right to completely take over the health of people by virtue of their profession. Now we are coming to see that the active cooperation of the patient with the best medical help that can be provided is an important ingredient in the struggle to regain or to maintain health.

2

Compassion, the Foundation of Care

So often we think that pastoral care of the sick can be given only by ministers. But "pastoral" care is that care for another given by any active and faith-filled member of the Christian community—the church—which has as its intention the continued life and growth in the gospel of the person cared for. Giving pastoral care to the sick means providing, in whatever form, the care that will prevent the distress, pain, or tragedy of illness from destroying the sick person's faith in Jesus Christ the Savior. Positively stated, pastoral care seeks not only to prevent sickness from destroying faith, but intends that even the suffering and tragedy of the sickness may be endured and used to strengthen faith in the abiding care of God. This is what the psalmist realized when he prayed: "Even though I walk through the valley of the shadow of death, I fear no evil; for thou art with me; thy rod and thy staff, they comfort me" (Ps. 23:4). In the imagery of the psalmist, care might well be the "rod and staff," which provide comfort as the sick person travels through the valley. This is what Paul realized when he rejoiced: "We know that in everything God works for good with those who love him, who are called according to his purpose. . . . For I am sure that neither death, nor life, nor angels, nor principalities, nor things present, nor things to come, nor powers, nor height, nor depth, nor anything else in all creation, will be able to separate us from the love of God in Christ Jesus our Lord" (Rom. 8:28, 38-39). Pastoral care fulfills its greatest potential when it assists another in arriving at that conviction. Such caring can be provided whether or not one is ordained.

Some years ago, shortly after we had moved out into the country to live, I was driving my old pickup into town. On the way I had a flat tire. There I was, stranded, because my old pickup didn't have a jack or tire wrench. I had found the spare tire, but it was useless without proper tools. I didn't know what to do, and it was a long walk into town. Then I discovered something about living in the country; before long someone in a beat-up old station wagon stopped and said, "Need any help?" Someone else knew what it was to be stranded on a country road and had stopped to help. So now when I'm driving on country roads, I too always stop to help. When we have been unexpectedly, graciously helped, we are naturally moved to help. Compassion received breeds compassion given.

Compassion is a hallmark of our discipleship and the sign of God's care for us. As the psalmist put it: "The Lord is gracious and merciful, slow to anger and abounding in steadfast love . . . his compassion is over all that he has made" (Ps. 145:8-9).

How does compassion work in human relationships? Why is it so important for a caring and healing relationship? It reflects and acts out our basic human condition under God, "who formed us in the womb," as Isaiah put it. This sense of our common humanity, the realization that "we are all in this together," " soul brothers and sisters," is basic to human caring. All thoughtful human caring must begin with this reaching out to the sufferer, by one who for the moment is stronger. This alignment forms a partnership in which the helper lends composure, courage, wisdom, and insight to the troubled person who shares fears, anxieties, pain, and a sense of powerlessness and despair. Pastoral care is providing compassion—being with people—just as God is "with us" in Jesus Christ (Emmanuel—Matt. 1:23). It is bringing the Christmas message of the God who came to be with us in our humanity. It is bringing the Lenten message of the God who suffers the consequences of our sin and guilt with us and for us on the cross so that we might be free. It is bringing the Easter message of the God who, in Christ, is totally with us, conquering all death and suffering.

Being compassionate

How do we do this? How can we ever so totally align ourselves alongside a sufferer so as to bear the suffering in the way that Jesus bore ours? First, by being willing to open ourselves to share another's burdens as Christ opened himself to share ours (Phil. 2:1-11). This means being willing to move from our secure and comfortable "normalcy" or "maturity" into the maelstrom of anxieties, doubts, pain, terror, and loneliness of the sick person's world. We do this almost naturally; we are moved with compassion when we see deep human suffering— unless we have hardened our hearts.

Along with exposing ourselves to another's suffering, another resource is helpful to move us alongside the sufferer: intercessory prayer. Intercessory prayer requires that we think or imagine ourselves into the needs and pain of another and then pray for the person with whom we are now in compassionate partnership.

As we move more deeply into this solidarity and provide continuing strength and comfort, we are ready to take the next step after intercessory prayer: careful listening and acceptance. Acceptance is the decision on the part of the caregiver that nothing the person receiving care does, says, or suffers shall drive us away. This is particularly important in dealing with the sick, because often there are physical expressions of illness—odors, blood, deformities—that are repulsive to visitors and to the patient. Compassion is the decision to hang in there no matter what.

Being compassionate is not usually a pleasant experience; it means hurting with another's hurt. If we allow ourselves to imagine what it must feel like to face an operation, suffer the pain of an auto accident, or whatever, we shrink from the experience. Here our intercessory prayer becomes also a prayer for strength, for it takes strength to move into another's suffering, to take it on ourselves, alongside the sufferer. Compassion truly is the cross of the Christian, the cross we are called to take up (Matt. 10:38) for the sake of our neighbor.

Compassion and acceptance do not mean simply agreeing with the person we are caring for. Nor do they involve simply being nonjudgmental. Acceptance moves deeper than mere understanding. It is not necessarily affirming or reassuring another that everything is going to be all right. And compassion is not just sympathy, feeling sorry for someone else who is suffering, and also, of course, being thankful that we are not suffering the same pain. Compassion and acceptance are *moving out into* another's pain and suffering, loneliness, and isolation, and helping to bear them.

Compassion requires disciplined sensitivity and the freedom and strength to be willing to allow ourselves to suffer another's hurt. The compassionate response is a demonstration of strength; it expresses our decision to stand by another, as God in his agape love steadfastly determines to stand by us.

But if compassion means only sharing the feelings of others, its effectiveness is limited. Compassion is not only joining in another's hurt; it also moves us to some action. When we participate in human tragedy—for example, when we share in the sudden tragic loss by a bedridden widow of her presumably healthy husband—we have the sense of wanting to do something. One of the clearest portraits of the true character of our Savior is the phrase that was used so many times to describe his participation in human tragedy: "he was moved with compassion" (Matt. 20:34; Mark 6:34; Luke 7:13). What a comfort to know that the Lord of life, the very Son of God, allowed his power to be directed by endless compassion! We can strive to do the same, to the degree that we are able.

Compassion then generates a sense of advocacy, of "being for," in a deeply moving way, the one for whom we are caring. Compassion must impel us to give special care, to exert some effort on behalf of the person cared for. What that will involve must be carefully governed by the needs of the sufferer, not by our own needs for a display of power or any kind of self-aggrandizement or manipulation. There is danger here, danger that we might be too impulsive in our sense of advocacy, too quick to solve problems that may be our own and not the sufferer's. If we are moved with compassion enough to remain faithful in our attention, listening concern, and unfailing acceptance, this is a beginning, but only a beginning. Like the Good Samaritan, we need to be disciplined to go beyond listening, to meet the obvious present needs of the sufferer as he or she shares them with us.

The moving power of compassion finally provides resources for responding to the needs of the other. The Good Samaritan was moved with compassion to tend the wounds of the victim and to provide continuing care. He used available resources to deal with what he compassionately perceived to be the needs of the of the robbed and beaten man. The compassionate response to cries from a drowning person must involve the ability to swim. So while we respond with compassion to the suffering of another, it is important that we are not overwhelmed by that suffering. If we are so overwhelmed, then we are impelled to deal with our own misery, to solve our own problems rather than caring for the other. Because we can't swim, we are then busy trying to save ourselves from drowning. Compassion, then, involves strength, courage, stability, skill, and discipline, along with the sensitive heart. This book is meant to help readers develop not only that compassionate heart but also the skill to provide compassionate care.

Learning this kind of compassion is difficult. But as Christians caring for the sick on behalf of the church, we are constantly aware that we rely not only on our own strength, courage, and faith, but on the promise of the Savior to be with us always, the promise that he sends the Comforter, the Spirit to enable us, guide us, and empower us as we venture into the anguish of others in his name.

Why is compassion so important in our care of the sick? The steadfast maintenance of the attitude of compassion makes it much easier for the sufferer to expose his or her worst self. There is no need to hide behind masks of artificial cheerfulness, no need to put on an act of bravery to cover up fear, no need to cover tears of pain with a stiff upper lip. The wounds of body and spirit need not be concealed. They can be shared, and in sharing, help and healing take place. This is important in the care of the ill, in which so often the tragic, painful, unpleasant side of human experience is exposed. The caregiver here shares something of the attitude of the faithful physician, who is not repulsed by anything having to do with our bodies, but is steadfast in caring. When such trust in the steadfast mercy of the caregiver takes place, true comfort and healing follow.

3

The Art of Listening

Two of the most significant ways we can be helpful to the sick person are by *presence* and by *understanding*. These two are really two sides of the same coin: *compassion*. We have already seen how compassion is the foundation of all pastoral care. Now we want to look at how one "does" compassion. (In the following accounts all names used are fictional. The incidents, however, are from actual experiences.)

The ministry of presence

Elderly Mrs. Charles was in the hospital for testing. She had been suffering from a reduced amount of oxygen to the brain, the nurse told the chaplain. The nurse also said that this was probably the first time Mrs. Charles had ever been in a hospital, and she was quite frightened.

As the visitor entered the room, Mrs. Charles was trying to head for the bathroom. She was a small woman in her early 70s. Her progress was slow because she was having difficulty maneuvering by herself. The visitor said: "My name is Jim. Can I give you some help?" She looked up at him somewhat vacantly. "Are you trying to get over to the bathroom?" Mrs. Charles made no response. "I would be more than happy to help you walk over there." Again, a pause and a stare. The conversation between the lay visitor and the patient went like this:

Visitor: Would you rather go back to bed? It appears as if this walking is making you rather weak. I could have the nurse called to help you, if you'd rather. *(Again, no response, but Mrs. Charles shuffled her feet as if she were going to turn around. I helped her and we slowly walked over to her bed.)* Would you like to sit in this chair, on your bed, or perhaps you'd prefer to lie down? *(Again, no vocal response, but she seemed to desire to sit on the edge of her bed. I assisted her to sit down. As she sat down, she took my hand with both of hers which forced me to sit beside her on the bed to keep from being off balance.)* Would you like for me to sit here with you or would you be more comfortable lying down, while I sat in the chair? *(Again, a long pause in which time there was no movement on her part. Her face gave the impression that she heard me, but that she was having a difficult time composing herself, or understanding quite what was going on.)* Perhaps I startled you when I first came in. My name is Jim. I'm from the chaplain's office. You indicated when you came into the hospital yesterday that you would like someone from the chaplain's office to stop by. Do you feel like visiting now, or should I give you a chance to rest and come back a little bit later?

Mrs. Charles: Thank you for coming. Now is fine.

Visitor: How are you feeling?

Mrs. Charles: (Her lower lip started quivering . . . reminding me very much of my two-year-old on the verge of crying. And a substantial pause followed.) I'm scared.

Visitor: It's all right to be scared. I'm here with you now. *(I accented this by squeezing her hand gently.)* Can you tell me what scares you? *(A long pause during which Mrs. Charles sobbed quietly to herself.)* It's all right to be scared—and to cry. *(Another long pause.)*

Mrs. Charles: I'm 70 years old and I've never been in a hospital before. *(She began quietly sobbing once again.)*

Visitor: If this is the first time you've ever been in a hospital, I can understand why you're scared. Do you understand why you're here?

The *presence* of the visitor, his being there beside her, holding her hand, sitting on the bed, is the most important act of ministry in this case. (Sitting on the patient's bed is ordinarily not done in hospital visiting, though in this visit we see that sometimes exceptions to this rule should be made.) "Being with" the sufferer (showing compassion) is the basis from which anything else in the visit may follow. The most eloquent form of this ministry of presence is recorded in the story of Job:

Now when Job's three friends heard of all this evil that had come upon him, they came each from his own place. . . . And when they saw him from afar, they did not recognize him; and they raised their voices and wept. . . . And they sat with him on the ground seven days and seven nights, and no one spoke a word to him, for they saw that his suffering was very great (Job 2:11-13).

Would any of us have the patience to sit for seven days without speaking a word? While this form of comforting was a cultural custom, it does say something important to us Americans who tend to zip in and zip out of conversations and relationships. We do not really know how to be with someone in suffering unless we take special pains to learn. In most Third World countries much more attention is paid to establishing a relationship or a good *connection* with someone before proceeding with the business of a conversation; a Zulu visiting a neighbor's *kraal* on a matter of business will sit at the gate for hours and come in only after being invited. Then, after being invited in, the visitor may spend additional hours inquiring about the health and well-being of every member of the family and talking about the weather or other things before coming to the point.

Establishing a good connection is important. Imagine yourself working on a difficult jigsaw puzzle. You have succeeded in putting together the edges of the puzzle, but now you're filling in the blue sky. All pieces seem the same, and none seem to fit. You are getting very frustrated. Then a friend comes along and sees what you are doing. After a minute or two of watching, she picks up one of the blue pieces and fits it exactly into the place you have been trying for hours to fill. Why is this bit of *help* so infuriating?

Now, imagine that instead of standing just a few minutes, your friend sits down and with you tries to fit in one piece after another. Eventually she says, "Let's try this one." This is genuine help, not a put-down, because real concern has been established by presence, by your friend sitting with you.

We Americans, with our notion that everything can be fixed, our belief that all we need to do is say something and everything will be all right, find it hard to learn the vital importance of presence. There are indeed times when nothing we say can help. Sometimes not even the words of Scripture help. What do we *say* to the parents of a 12-year-old who has just been killed by a drunken driver? What *words* of Scripture or anything else can help? Words can't help. What can is the Emmanuel—God-with-us—suffering alongside, silently demonstrated by the handclasp or the embrace of another caring person. Just knowing that another person cares deeply helps. We cannot always explain how.

Listening

To be truly effective, however, presence needs to be more than just being there—as the story of Job's friends makes clear. Presence must involve being there *with compassion*—the willingness and the freedom to enter into the suffering of the other, even when we cannot fix it. This means we must have the capacity to listen and to hear as the other expresses anguish, confusion, anger, or pain, without attempting to counteract, argue, or fix in such a way as to make the anger go away. Sometimes a word can erase anguish, as in the case of a word of pardon or of love, but when it comes to physical pain or anguish, this is not usually true. Let's listen to a visitor who tries to fix things with argumentative responses.

The student chaplain is visiting 78-year-old Mrs. Carlson, who has lived alone since her husband died a year ago. she currently is hospitalized with a fractured hip. Mrs. Carlson has a son and daughter in a nearby city who do not want her living alone anymore. They have asked for someone from the church to visit her.

Visitor: I'm Chris Smith. I heard from your daughter you were here.
Mrs. Carlson: Please come in.

Visitor: How are you feeling?

Mrs. Carlson: Do you know my daughter?

Visitor: Yes.

Mrs. Carlson: She wants me to give up my home and move into an old folks' home. She wants me to give up everything I own. *(She becomes agitated.)*

Visitor: I'm sure your daughter is only looking out for you.

Mrs. Carlson: She wants me to move!

Visitor: Maybe because you'll get better care.

Mrs. Carlson: I'm not sick. As soon as this hip heals, I can take care of myself.

Visitor: Your daughter told me that your home is very beautiful, but that there are steps that are very steep and dangerous.

Mrs. Carlson (silent for a moment): I do have trouble getting around, but when I need help I can call my daughter or my son to help me.

Visitor: Does she come?

Mrs. Carlson: No, when I need them most, they are too busy. I don't want to move. *(She goes on to talk about her home, the pride she takes in it, how she cherishes many of the beautiful things she has.)*

Visitor: Your possessions mean a lot to you, don't they?

Mrs. Carlson (sadly): That's all I have.

We can quickly see what has happened if we ask the question, "In whose presence was the visitor?" It is quite clear that the visitor was really being with the daughter rather than with Mrs. Carlson. We are not disputing the daughter's logic or her love—but we have here a situation in which the visitor did not really *listen* to the person she was visiting. Instead, she argued. This visit continued in much the same vein until Mrs. Carlson finally turned away and looked out the window saying, "Everyone is against me."

The visitor is frequently in a situation like this when it appears that he or she must take sides. The alternative is to listen to all sides and then, perhaps, if the opportunity presents itself, to help the people involved listen to and hear each other. Listening is not trying to convince someone.

How does one listen and really hear? In the literature of counseling, this is sometimes called *active listening* or *empathy*. The technique becomes obvious when we perceive clearly what the purpose of listening is. Simply put, that purpose is to sit beside another in his or her situation (as in Job's story), or, in the Native American phrase, "to walk a mile in his moccasins." It is, as the word *empathy* indicates, to "feel into." *Listening* is to be *truly present* with another by hearing his or her plight without giving in to our temptation to counteract, to correct, to change, to inform, to teach, or to do anything. There is often a place for any or all of these functions—but they best occur *after* listening has taken place.

We listen when we are willing and able to enter into the feeling-world of another. We really experience how it feels. We provide the space, the full freedom, for the other to express his or her feelings and thus to reveal to us the feeling world in which he or she is now suffering and struggling.

The careful listener will train the ear for "feeling words" like *afraid, happy, worried, angry, hurt, upset,* instead of thinking words like *anxious, hostile, disturbed, distressed.* These thinking words describe rather than convey genuine feelings.

It is difficult to grasp this basic technique of expressing our own or hearing others' genuine *feelings*. This is true, in part, because to show how we genuinely feel about something is to reveal ourselves, and this always involves the risk of indifference, ridicule, or outright rejection. These are much more threatening than simple misunderstanding, which can always be explained or clarified. To express feelings is to express vulnerability. Therefore, we must be able to trust that the persons to whom we express our real feelings will not turn their backs on us. This is particularly important when the feelings being expressed are negative feelings of pain, anguish, fear, and worry—the feelings usually involved in being sick. Being sick and expressing the feelings of sickness is always thought of as weakness, insufficiency, or guilt by the sick person. This is reinforced by society which assigns this "weakness" role to the invalid. (Note the etymology of that word: *in-valid* = *not valid.*)

For all of these reasons, then, there must be a relationship of genuine compassion and caring before real feelings will be expressed. Listening is not primarily a technique used indiscriminately; it becomes effective only when there is first the basic relationship of compassion, the genuine desire to be alongside another.

The *skill* of hearing feelings, which also demonstrates a *willingness* to hear feelings, does much to build a relationship of compassion and trust. It says to the sick person, "This visitor wants to hear how I really feel."

Fact and meaning

When listening it is helpful to make a distinction between *facts* and *meaning*. Though these two components of verbal communication are usually more or less fused there is a difference between them. What we call *facts* are the "what has happened to me" information. What we call *meaning* is the "how what has happened to me makes me feel," or the *significance* of what is happening to me. When we are listening for feelings, we are not listening only for emotions. Behind those emotions of fear, anguish, and pain are deeper dimensions. The following dialog illustrates this point.

Mrs. Krause is 79 years old, a widow and a devout church member. She had been admitted through the emergency room of the hospital for cardiac care.

Visitor: I wanted to stop by and check on how you were doing.

Mrs. Krause: I'm doing all right now. God didn't take me yet.

Visitor: You have had problems with your heart?

Mrs. Krause: Yes, I had chest pains again. I thought for sure that this was the time, but it wasn't. God isn't ready for me yet.

Visitor: You've had these pains before?

Note here the close fusion of fact and content. Note, too, how the visitor tends to respond to the meaning rather than the feeling. To Mrs. Krause having pains in her chest *means* death. That is the primary meaning, together with her feelings about death. From this little excerpt we can get a fairly good glimpse of how she *feels* about death, so we do not need to ask the fatuous question, "How do you feel about that?" She feels some fear but also some anticipation. The *facts* about her dying are that she knows she is in the Lord's hands; death *means* to her that God will take her in a special way. Thus the listener carefully sifts facts and meaning and then chooses to respond to either or both. To respond to meaning will usually quickly deepen the relationship between the partners in communication. Let us listen to Mrs. Krause a little longer as we learn to distinguish facts and meaning.

Mrs. Krause: I keep praying for God to take me. I've suffered for many years, and there is no reason for me to stay on this earth. I've had a good life. If only God would take me!

Facts: She prays. She has suffered. She feels there is no more reason for her to continue living. She is appreciative of a good life. She believes in God. Her conception of death is that God takes her in some way.

Meaning: Prayer is the behavior of *trust* for her. She appreciates the life she has had. She feels comfortable in God's presence. She has not directly expressed what the suffering has meant for her, but we can conjecture that she suffers patiently, without complaining. She may feel that it is wrong to complain, but we do not know this without more careful listening.

We don't usually analyze conversation in this detailed fashion, but for the visitor who wishes really to understand others, it is important to make this sort of analysis as an exercise in developing the skill of listening. As we detail the content of what Mrs. Krause is saying, we begin to come close to what life is really like for her in this moment. We "get beneath the skin" so to speak, of her experience. We are beginning to be compassionate.

As we begin to hear and distinguish fact and meaning, we must make some sensitive decisions about how to proceed with the conversation. Mrs. Sullivan illustrates that for us in a conversation with a lay visitor from her congregation.

Visitor: You look good. What is it that the doctors are testing for?

Mrs. Sullivan: Well, I have rheumatoid arthritis, you know, pretty bad at times, particularly in my legs. They wanted to run some tests to find out if anything else might be the matter. I've been here several days now, and they've run scans for just about everything. They wouldn't let me eat anything last night or this morning and had to clean me out good last night so they could run scans today. They've looked at just about everything they can, it seems.

Here Mrs. Sullivan is reporting largely factual information about what is happening to her, much the same as she might report to a newspaper reporter. But we can detect meanings in what she is saying: She is beginning to wonder about all those tests. We can almost hear her asking, "It can't all be just for arthritis. Is there something else wrong?" She may be afraid that something more serious is involved, although we do not yet know this for certain.

In instances like this, the visitor has to make a strategic decision. Should he or she continue being the "reporter," until Mrs. Sullivan feels more comfortable? Or, should the visitor cautiously make it possible for Mrs. Sullivan to begin to verbalize some of the emotional content that seems to lie just beneath the surface of the conversation? A response that would do the latter might be: "You're beginning to wonder what the meaning of all these different scans might be?" or "You're beginning to wonder whether this is all for arthritis?" or "You're beginning to feel impatient about all these tests?" or "You wish the doctors would tell you why they are doing all these tests?"

There is no one right word to say. The appropriate response depends on the level of our perceptiveness and what we and the person we are visiting wish to accomplish with our conversation.

In developing the skill to perceive what the patient is experiencing and what it means to him or her, it is helpful to learn to assess quickly the meaning of what is being said with a few precise feeling words.

In the following dialog, note—and possibly even write down for yourself—the *facts* and *meanings* in each patient response.

The patient being visited, Mr. Thomas, is a male, about 30 years old, paralyzed from the waist down.

Visitor: Hi! I'm Mary from the Protestant Chaplain's office. I stopped by to see how you are doing.

Mr. Thomas: Fine.

Visitor: Feeling OK?

Mr. Thomas: I'm paralyzed from about here down *(indicates middle of his chest).* My arms ache, all through here—especially my right arm. I'm sort of paralyzed under my arm here. I can't feel anything.

Visitor: Oh!

Mr. Thomas: All I can do is ache. I can't get much sleep. I have to lie on either one side or the other all the time. I have a big sore on my back.

Visitor: Makes it kind of tough because you're always lying on your arm.

Mr. Thomas: Yes, my arms get so tired from lying on them all the time.

Visitor: Can you turn yourself or does somebody turn you?

Mr. Thomas: Well, usually I have to be turned.

Visitor: Is it important to be turned often?

Mr. Thomas: Yes, it is. I get this thing over me to keep the blankets off my sore. If that wasn't there, I'd really stink. Couldn't even stand myself.

Visitor: That sore's pretty bad, eh? Is it a bed sore?

Mr. Thomas: Yeah, I guess that's what it is. That's why I have to keep turning or I'll get them all over me. They don't care much in here. The nurses don't know anything about it. Half the time they don't turn me often enough. I can't do anything.

Visitor: You don't think you're getting the kind of care you need?

Mr. Thomas: No. If I could only get some physical therapy, I could do something. You see, I got into trouble in Brownsville. A cop shot me in the back. The bullet went in along my side some place, but it hit my spine. That's why I'm paralyzed. Now I'm getting worse and worse. I've got to have some help.

Visitor: You think if you got the proper physical therapy, you could pull out of this pretty well?

Mr. Thomas: I know I could. I know what they were doing for me at the other hospital. Why am I here? I can't do any more crimes. I can't even walk. I know I'll never be able to walk again, but I don't mind. I know I did wrong, and I owe a debt to society, but I can never pay it back like this. I can never learn to support myself. Justice, it's a funny thing.

Now reread the dialog and note the meanings expressed or implied in the visitor's responses. How they match will tell you how compassionate the visitor is.

The visitor's feelings

In addition to developing a sensitive ear for the feelings and meanings being expressed by the patient, the visitor also needs to monitor his or her own feelings and reactions to what the patient looks like, smells like, how the hospital or sick room affects one, the pain the patient is suffering, and the general situation of the patient. In fact, we as visitors are sensitive instruments responding to what others around us are experiencing. So, in the visit above, we might expect the visitor to respond with some anger about the apparent lack of care that the patient is receiving, the callousness of the nurse, or of the social-justice system that does nothing to rehabilitate a person so he can redeem his debt to society. Or, we might react with a sense of justice, feeling that he is getting what he deserved. Our temptation often is to react and respond to our *own* feelings as visitors, rather than to respond to the feelings or content of what the patient is saying and experiencing.

In the visit recorded above, for example, the visitor might well respond with some indignation: "Well, you certainly are getting a raw deal. The hospital ought to see to it that you get the kind of rehabilitation you need so that you can learn a trade and support yourself. I think it's terrible the way you have to lie and literally rot like this." If we are tempted to respond in this fashion, we need to think carefully about how this response to our own personal feelings would be of help to the patient. That must be our primary concern: to consider how we can be helpful to another, rather than to satisfy our own feelings of righteousness, anger, pity, or even sympathy. When we respond to our own feelings, the bridge of compassion is broken; we are no longer with the patient. We are ruminating with ourselves, even as the patient is ruminating with himself, and no healing relationship is being built.

We can see the interplay of factual material, emotional content, and visitor response if we look at a portion of an interview in some detail, analyzing carefully each statement and response.

The patient, Mr. Wilson, is a 48-year-old man, who has listed himself as divorced and a former professional athlete. He was injured in a fall from a scaffolding on which he was working. As a consequence of this fall, he had to have a leg amputated.

Visitor: Good morning. Do you remember me? I visited you last week.

Remember that in a hospital countless people troop in and out of the patient's room daily so the patient may well not remember. To ask if he or she does may be putting the patient on the spot.

Mr. Wilson: Yes, I remember.
Visitor: Well, how are you doing since I last saw you?
Mr. Wilson: I'll be leaving the hospital soon.

The sensitive visitor will listen here for the tone of voice which will give a better indication of what the patient is feeling. It sounds like good news, and there seems to be some real elation about it. Note the close interplay of fact and meaning here.

Visitor: Do you have family and friends who will look after you?

This is a solicitous question, but it ignores almost entirely the feeling of elation and sense of accomplishment the patient has shared. This information-seeking question centers entirely on the factual information in the patient's life. It would have been better to respond to both facts and emotional content, as in a response like, "You sound pretty elated about that possibility. Will there be people at home to look after you?"

Mr. Wilson: Yes. Some of my children live in Columbus and visit me regularly. *(Pause.)* How long will you be working here?

Notice how the patient shifted the attention to the visitor. The mood of the visit has cooled down because the visitor ignored the patient's feelings of joy expressed earlier. The visitor now has to direct the conversation back to the patient's life.

Visitor (responds with appropriate information to the patient's inquiry, and then goes on): Tell me, has it been difficult for you to be confined to a wheelchair?

Such a direct approach to the issue should not be attempted unless the relationship itself is quite strong. Here it is important that the patient know the visitor is asking this blunt question not out of idle curiosity but from a genuine desire to be helpful. Since this is the second time the visitor has seen the patient, we assume that the relationship is strong enough. Here we see the importance of *presence* and *compassion* as foundations.

Mr. Wilson: I was always an active man. Do you know that I was one of the top football players in the country? I also worked as a carpenter, so it has been hard not being able to work. I also wish I could get around more when I see children playing in the summertime.

Notice here how much of himself the patient has revealed—his feeling of pride in his athletic life, his frustration at not being able to be physically active, his sensitivity to children, and his joy of life—all of which are threatened by his loss. We begin to get a real feeling of what it means to him to lose his leg.

Visitor: How did you become paralyzed?

All of what the patient has said about himself is overlooked as the visitor pursues the goal of getting "all the facts." We know by now that "all the facts" are not really the important thing here.

One of the most common mistakes of visiting the sick is failing to work with the material that people share as they express themselves. In this visit the visitor should work with the rich variety of content that Mr. Wilson has shared, instead of leapfrogging ahead for still more historical data. There are a variety of ways in which the visitor might have done this. For example, the visitor might have said: "It's really hard for you to sit on the sidelines and watch others be active, especially the children," or, "You miss very much not being able to be energetic and active," or, "You took a lot of pride in being a fine athlete, and now you have to say good-bye to all of this as you sit on the sidelines and watch."

But let us go back to the conversation.

Mr. Wilson (goes on to explain how he became paralyzed): It happened when I was working on the third floor of a building. The ladder I was using gave way. I

gripped the gutters, but they broke, and I fell on a
wooden shed near the building. I bounded off the
shed and fell to the ground.

Notice the candid, matter-of-fact way he reports the
facts. He knows by now that the visitor wants facts and
is not so much concerned for how he feels, so he gives
facts. Often we wonder why visits or conversations seem
so cold and matter-of-fact. It may be because we don't
really respond to the feelings and meanings that persons
have expressed to us.

The visitor senses this and wants to correct it and attempts to do so.

Visitor: Did you see your life rushing before you as you
    fell?

In addition to trying to get at what it must have felt
like to fall from that height, the visitor is again responding to his own feelings of curiosity to check out a myth
that he has heard about the moments before dying. At
a point like this, it might be appropriate to do a bit of
imagining, putting ourselves into the other's place with
a response like: "I can imagine that must have been a
horrifying experience to fall that distance."

Mr. Wilson: Yes, many thoughts came to my mind, but
    I blacked out once I hit the shed.
Visitor: How serious were your injuries?
Mr. Wilson. Well, I was paralyzed from the waist down
    and either had to use a wheelchair or crutches to
    get around.

Again, he reports the fact to the visitor, almost as if
he were talking to an insurance investigator. Again, the

visitor wants to get it off that level, and he again attempts to do it by a question, rather than the more appropriate way of doing it—by using the self-revelations the patient has already shared.

Visitor: Did you ever wonder why God allowed this to happen to you?

Mr. Wilson: Yes, I have thought about this often. I don't think that was the Lord who did this to me. It was Satan. You see, I was going out with another woman when I was still married to my wife. So basically, I was doing Satan's will and not God's will. I had committed my life to the ways of Satan, and he caused me to have this accident.

We note the theological contradiction here, but that should not be our central concern right now. Note rather, the expression of a sense of guilt, though it is couched again in *factual* terms. It is possible that Mr. Wilson does not feel free to share with the visitor his personal sense of shame and remorse.

Visitor: Do you think it is correct to say that? Is it not that we live in a world where accidents can happen? We can't really put the blame on God or Satan.

Many people with a faith perspective fall into the trap of theological argument. In this dialog the important thing is not correct theology, but the sense of remorse and guilt Mr. Wilson feels and what help we bring for this through the gospel. We will discuss this particular issue more in detail in the chapter on the spiritual and theological resources of the pastoral visitor.

From this dialog, we can see how the sensitive ear can quickly get to know a person through the readiness with which people reveal themselves. We also see how delicately we must handle the self-revelations of people, or they will quickly hide behind the facade of the facts.

Why is it so important to respond to the meanings of experience and to feelings as we listen to the sick?

1. It demonstrates that we are serious about moving alongside the person we are listening to, struggling to enter into his or her experience.

2. Our response demonstrates that we *do* understand to some limited extent what their experience of illness is doing to them. It demonstrates this understanding far more clearly than saying, "I understand."

3. Our entering into their feelings and sharing the meaning of illness also provides immediate, strong support and lays the foundation for further support that might be provided at a later time.

4. Listening for feelings and responding to them also communicates the implicit message that we are not offended, disturbed, unsettled, or shocked by strong feelings. Instead, we accept them. Responding with accurate empathy to the feelings expressed gives permission to the person to express more fully and clearly what he or she is struggling to come to terms with. In thus focusing on feelings, we are providing the first step in the eventual integration of feelings and meaning, which establishes an important base for spiritual and emotional growth to come.

Empathic and skillful dealing with feelings is an important and necessary *first step* in building a good pastoral relationship, establishing solidarity with the person we are visiting, and laying the groundwork for further pastoral work—which we will consider in the following chapters.

4

The Hospital Visit

It's time now to make a hospital visit. How shall we enter that strange world of a hospital? We are not the patient, neither are we anxious family members of the one who is sick. How can we come as concerned friends, representatives of the family of God, someone who wants to understand, to give support and encouragement and to be compassionate? What should we do and not do?

Getting ready for the visit

To begin, it is important to know as much as you can about the person whom you are going to visit. It is especially important to know something of the person's home and family life, if possible. Where does the person fit into the family—as parent, child, aunt, uncle, or grandparent? How is the family affected by the person's illness? As a fellow member of the congregation it is likely that you will know much of this from your regular contact or knowledge of the patient and the family. Often the pastor can fill in important information without breaking personal confidences.

It also is helpful if you can learn something of the nature of the person's illness. However, be very careful not to invade the privacy of the patient or the family when getting this information. Your concern here is not just to satisfy your curiosity, but to gather only such information as will help you in being helpful to the person you are going to care for by your visit. You have a right only to such information as you can helpfully use in your care for the patient. It is not always easy to know what will be useful in this way, but remember to keep your personal curiosity in check as you seek helpful information.

It also is important not to let yourself become intimidated by the information you gather. Here you will have to carefully monitor your own attitudes about being sick and even about certain illnesses. If, for example, you have lost a close member of your family as a result of cancer, and you still have strong fears about cancer, or have some unresolved feelings of grief about the death of your loved one, you may be intimidated by the diagnosis of cancer and your helpfulness may be hampered. This may be because you will be more preoccupied with your own feelings about cancer and thus insensitive to the patient. Some of my students have lost family members to a heart attack and have been afraid that they, too, might have a heart attack because it runs in the family. So it has been very difficult for them to be attentive, to give support and hope to a patient with heart disease. Only after they recognized their own fears and dealt with them at least to some extent could they be compassionate visitors.

At the hospital

We have arrived at the hospital to visit Miss Yost, an elderly member in the congregation, long active in the church. She has been visited by the pastor of the congregation, and now you are amplifying this pastoral relationship with your own visit.

After you have found out the patient's room number, you go to the appropriate floor. Your first stop is at the nurses' charge desk—the place where the charts for all the patients on the floor are kept. Your purpose here is to introduce yourself as a visitor for the patient. The nurse may want to know whether you are a member of the family, a friend, or a special visitor. It may, therefore, be helpful to introduce yourself as a delegated congregational visitor making your visit at the request of the pastor and under his or her supervision. Knowing that you have a professional as well as personal concern for the patient may allow the nurse to be more specific and helpful in the information he or she may share with you about the patient.

You may then ask the nurse, "Is there anything I ought to know about the patient's condition before I go in to visit?" Give some care how you word the request for information so that you do not put the nurse on the spot. You should not ask the nurse to violate professional and ethical responsibility to guard the privacy of the patient. Be careful not to demand information as though you have a right to it. Allow the nurse to use professional judgment as to how much or what type of information can be shared with you. As you make more visits in the hospital and the staff and nurses get to know you and whom you represent, and as they find that your work with patients is helpful and professional, they will feel free to entrust you with more specific information when that could be helpful to you, the patient, and your work.

Do not forget to ask if it is all right to go into the patient's room for the visit. The nurse may want to check beforehand. In this way you avoid blundering into what can be embarrassing situations for the patient or yourself.

As you walk down the hallway to the hospital room, pause a moment before you go into the room and pray a silent prayer of intercession for the person you are about to visit. Pray also that you will be an instrument of God's compassion and peace, that you will be sensitive to the fears, hopes, joys, and anxieties of the patient. Such a prayer is healing for the patient and helpful to you, making you more sensitive and alert, a ready instrument of the Spirit of God who will guide you through the visit.

You may also wish to pause a moment before making the visit to reflect on all the information you now have about the patient and what this might suggest to you by way of special sensitivity on your part. You know that Miss Yost, being an active member of the congregation, will welcome a visit by a representative of the congregation. Since she is normally an active person, she may be distressed at not being able to be up and around. Since you know she is in for medical observation, she may be concerned, perhaps even a bit alarmed, about the findings. These sensitivities on your part, along with your prayer, help you to be especially attuned to concentrating on the needs of the patient herself and help you put your own concerns in the background.

Beginning and ending the visit

As you enter the room, practice the skill of careful observation. Take a mental photograph of the patient's demeanor or mood, the state of the bed, the articles on the bedside table, the appearance of the patient. This can tell you a great deal about how the patient is at the time of your visit and can eliminate many unnecessary questions. For example, because Miss Yost has been long active in the congregation, you might expect that she has a number of get-well cards and perhaps some flowers in her room. But as you enter the doorway, you see only one card on the bedside table and no flowers.

This may suggest several things, but be careful not to jump to premature conclusions. It may suggest that no one in the congregation knows she is in the hospital. It probably suggests that she is a bit lonely and feels just a bit forgotten by everyone. But it may also suggest that the nurse's aide has just cleaned the room, put all the old cards away and thrown away wilted flowers, and the one card has just arrived. Whatever the case, by observing this, you are sensitized to several possible moods of the patient. You may want to comment on the one card in such a way as to allow the patient to share what her situation is. In the original visit with Miss Yost, the visitor noted:

> As I knocked and entered the room, Miss Yost was sitting up in bed in a room she shared with two other women, one of whom was absent at the time. She appeared to be in good spirits, her hair was combed and it was obvious that she was not bedridden, nor did she appear in any way to be ailing.

When visiting women, it is helpful to note details of makeup; this is often a very good indicator of mood.

The conversation begins:

Visitor: Hello, Miss Yost. I'm Louise Nelson. We attend the same church.

Miss Yost: Oh, hi, Louise. I didn't recognize you when you first walked in.

Visitor: I'm helping the pastor make calls on the sick. I learned you were here so I wanted to be sure to see you. How are you doing?

It is important to clarify your role, particularly with people who may not know you personally. This assures them of your purpose in making the visit.

Generally, it is better not to ask patients, "How are you feeling?" because they are likely to answer in a way that will not make them sound like complainers, so they will say something like "fine" or "all right," and you really won't get helpful information. It is better to indicate your special concern for them in a more general way, such as this visitor used, or by asking, "How are things going for you today?" or, "Did you have a good night?" Learn to ask questions that encourage the patient to say more than yes or no.

We have discussed in the previous chapter how to listen to—how to be with—a patient during a hospital visit. How does the visit conclude?

Visitor: I'm a little concerned that I might be wearing you out a bit. You may be a bit more tired after all those tests than you've told me.

Miss Yost: I think you're right, but I'm sure glad you stopped by.

Always be sensitive to the patient's easy tiring. A hospital visit should rarely last as long as a visit in someone's home. Remember that illness saps energies and makes one tire easily.

Visitor: Let's join together in a brief prayer before I go.
Miss Yost: Yes, please.
Visitor (taking her hand): Our heavenly Father, we come
before you in thanks for the gift of life that we share
with each other and also for the gift of life that is
your gift through Jesus Christ. We don't know the
why of Miss Yost's being in the hospital or the outcome of the tests, but you know. So we trust in you
to care for her, and for the doctors and the nurses.
As Miss Yost finds the results of the tests, we pray
that they may show a clean bill of health. If it should
be otherwise, we pray for your strength so that we
might understand and be comforted. You are our
Father, and we trust you to care for us.

It is usually helpful to touch the patient in this way at some time in the visit or during the prayer. It would have been better if the visitor and Miss Yost had talked a bit together about possible results of the tests, rather than mentioning it only in the prayer. We will discuss this more fully in the next chapter.

The visitor might add: "I hope you're already headed for home, but if not, I'll stop by again on Thursday morning." It is often helpful to let the person know when you plan to visit again. But be sure you follow through!

Reflect on your visit

One of the most important ways of learning how to make effective hospital visits is to write up a report for yourself. In that way you can examine more carefully what you have done, what the patient is saying, and the concerns being expressed by what the patient says. You can also learn much from your mistakes.

Your analysis should deal with these questions: (1) What is the patient experiencing, and how does he or she feel about it? What meaning does the patient find for the experiences he or she is going through? What is he or she willing to talk about, and what is avoided? (2) What are the faith issues the patient's situation identifies? What implications for the spiritual life of the patient are being raised? How can the visitor or the pastor deal with these most helpfully? (3) What should be given careful attention for the next hospital or home visit? What other members of the family or congregation might be involved to help the patient? What special needs of the patient (such as visits from friends, finances, provisions for returning home) should be attended to? How can the congregation be most helpful?

As an exercise for yourself, try to write out an analysis of the visit that has been reported here, answering the above questions. Note how this analysis becomes a helpful guide for your next visit with the person. Giving careful attention to some of the details mentioned here does much to help you become a skilled visitor.

Keeping confidences

One of the important aspects of being sick in the hospital is the issue of personal privacy. The hospital seems to be a place where all privacy is stripped away. This is especially true of physical privacy. Therefore, it is all the more important that we preserve personal emotional and spiritual privacy as carefully as possible.

Because you are a special visitor for the congregation, people may ask you, "How is Miss Yost getting along?"

It is appropriate to share some news about the people you will be visiting so that the congregation and friends can feel some contact with them. The people you will be visiting know that you will be talking to members of the congregation, and they too want to maintain contact with friends, family, and the congregation. But because of this, the patient may also be hesitant to reveal to you personal, intimate, and especially troubling concerns, for fear that you will "gossip" these all over the congregation. Therefore, you need to be very careful about preserving the privacy of the patient, while still keeping him or her in contact with family and congregation.

When you are asked about the well-being of someone you have been visiting, it is wise to ask yourself first of all, "Does what I share preserve the privacy and integrity of my friend, the patient?" By doing so, you will not reveal anything that would be embarrassing or demeaning to the patient. But you may not always be the best judge of what might be embarrassing to the patient. If you have any doubts as to what should be shared or not, ask the patient, "Do you mind if I tell the members of your family or the congregation how you are getting on?" Or you might ask, "What should I tell the members of the congregation or your family about how you are getting along?" In this way you are communicating to the person your intention to be careful about his or her confidence, that you can be trusted not to spread gossip. With this assurance the patient will come to take you as a special confidant, and you will find that you can quite often be much more helpful to him or her.

In general, then, adopt the principle that everything shared in personal conversation between you and the patient in the sickroom is to be kept in confidence, unless you have the permission of that person to talk to others about it. If congregation or family wants to know how things are going, answer in a general way, without revealing *any* special details, unless you have the patient's permission to do otherwise. In the visit with Mrs. Sullivan (Chapter 3) such a general answer might be: "She's feeling quite well and expects to be going home soon." You would *not* tell anyone that "She is awaiting the outcome of several tests and is quite worried about them." To reveal this would give rise to all kinds of speculations and rumors about what might be happening to Mrs. Sullivan, and would make her uncomfortable and perhaps embarrassed about being worried, because in the minds of many, a good Christian is not supposed to worry.

When to share information with the pastor can become a special issue. It may well be helpful for the pastor to know that Mrs. Sullivan is becoming anxious, because the pastor is in a special professional and personal position to help her with her worries. It may also be that you can help her with her worries, but you need some more guidance or suggestions from the pastor. In this instance, as well, it is always wisest to ask Mrs. Sullivan, "Do you mind if I share with the pastor your feelings about the test findings?" It might even be helpful to explain why you would want to do this. The pastor knows that when you share this intimate information, he or she is also bound by the pledge of confidentiality and should not reveal this information to anyone else without permission. If you are a lay visitor for the sick in your congregation, you and your pastor will want to work out some means by which the pastor knows whom you are seeing and can give you whatever specialized help, guidance, or support you might need. You and your pastor, along with other hospital visitors in your congregation, could meet regularly to talk and think and pray together about your work with members who are ill and home-bound. But as you do, always keep in mind that every-thing the patients have shared with you in conversation is held in sacred trust. You will want to be true to that trust.

Family members often feel that they have a special right to all information about the people you will be visiting. In a sense this is true, but here again you have to weigh carefully what you can share with them and what you cannot. A safe rule is, when in doubt, always ask the permission of the patient for the freedom to share information, even with family. There will be some in-stances when you feel the family not only has a right, but *should* know what is going on with the patient, but the patient does not want you to share information with them. This frequently happens when the test results are bad, or when the condition is serious or even terminal. Even here you are bound by the rules of confidentiality. But you will perhaps want to help the patient become free to share the difficult news with the family so they can share the burden of anxiety. You can also be guided by another principle: how will the information I am shar-ing be helpful to the patient? How can the people to whom I am giving the information (with the patient's consent) be more helpful to the patient because they have the information? How can sharing the information help the entire congregation be more compassionate and caring to the patient?

The rule of confidentiality may seem at times to re-quire you to be untruthful to those who ask about the welfare of a patient. This need not be so. All you have to do is to say, "I'm sorry, but the conversations I have with people I visit are confidential. I cannot tell you any more without the permission of the patient." In this way the person who is asking you will know that you are someone who wants to be trusted. They will also feel more confident in you if you visit *them* in the hospital. And they will know, too, that your uppermost concern is the well-being of the person you are seeing.

The hospital is a specialized world, but it need not be frightening for you or for the patients you see. Keep in mind always that your fundamental intention is to have a friendly, warm, and personal conversation with the person you are seeing—no more and no less. If you learn to listen carefully to what the other person is saying to you, you will also discover how to respond in a way that can be most healing.

Be ready to become a part of the healing team

There is a new ferment among the various professions of the healing arts today. This is due in part to the work of some pioneer Lutheran pastors and chaplains, notably Dr. Granger E. Westberg who has pioneered open professional communication between physician and pastors. Recently he has promoted parish-centered health care units and "health care cabinets." Much work still needs to be done to help bridge the gap that still, unfortunately, exists between highly technological medicine and the personal and pastoral work of persons. For further information on this subject, you may want to read Dr. Westberg's books, *Minister and Doctor Meet*, (New York, Harper and Row, 1961) and *Nurse, Pastor and Patient* (information to come). The name *holistic health care* has frequently been given to this movement. The Wheatridge Foundation also has become especially interested in this area.

One of the sources of this new ferment is the growing disenchantment on the part of general society with the depersonalized effect of much of modern technological medicine. The pace of technological medicine, with the necessity of increasingly narrow specialization, has often resulted in the depersonalization that is generally deplored. Medical schools are aware of the problem, and one response is the creation of departments of family medicine.

A second source of this ferment is the waning of the physician's authority over the care of the patient in favor of a more egalitarian or team approach. Many hospitals now provide incoming patients with a patient's bill of rights, which is a response to consumer protection and the patient's right to know. The climate of adversary medicine and excessive malpractice suits are a negative aspect of this trend. The postitive values are that an increasing sensitivity to the *human dimensions of medicine* is developing. The church should be a staunch supporter of this trend.

A third source of this new ferment in health care arises from the concepts of healing and ministry that reach beyond the concepts of both traditional psychosomatic medicine and spiritual healing. Dr. W. S. Reed is reported as having said, "In many ways medicine is a ministry; we're more than just doctors." Physicians and nurses, pastors and lay pastoral visitors all are now centering more attention on *care,* without doing so at the expense of *cure.*

It can be exciting to you, as a lay pastoral visitor, to enter this arena of care and cure in a climate of concern for increasing humanity in medicine and the increasing desire for closer cooperation between physician, those concerned for spiritual care, and society itself. You, therefore, can be a welcome member of the healing team.

The healing team

Most modern hospitals use the healing-team concept in caring for patients. This is the close cooperation between doctors on the hospital staff, (including surgeons, interns, psychiatrists, anesthesiologists, and other specialists), nurses of all specialities, respiratory therapists, physical therapists, occupational therapists, and other members of the allied health professions, dietitians, nursing assistants, and housekeeping staff. If there is a chaplain in the hospital, he or she is frequently included. These members of the healing team will keep frequent and close contact with each other to communicate about what they are doing for the patient, their clinical and diagnostic impressions, and their plans and suggestions for future treatment. This is done by means of conferences—rounds—and by careful recording on the patient's medical chart. As a general rule the patient's medical chart is off limits for the visitor who is not part of the hospital staff, whether that person is the pastor or the lay parish visitor. This is not to say, however, that the visitor cannot or should not be in some way involved in the healing team effort. Frequently, however, the initiative to make one's contribution to the healing team effort has to come from the visitor. Such efforts are usually welcomed by the team members. The channels of communication between parish visitor and the physician or other members of the hospital's healing team may be a verbal message via the charge nurse, a written memo, or a telephone call.

Pastor James Schmidt had been visiting Mrs. Wilkins often during the past three weeks. It was evident that Mrs. Wilkins' chances for recovery were slim because of possible brain damage. Mrs. Wilkins' husband, Fred, was waiting for the results of an electroencephalogram. Pastor Schmidt had visited Mrs. Wilkins two days prior to this telephone call to the doctor.

Dr. Brown: Hello?

Pastor Schmidt: Hello, this is James Schmidt. I'm Henrietta Wilkins' pastor.

Dr. Brown: Oh, yes.

Pastor Schmidt: I've been spending a good deal of time visiting with Mrs. Wilkins' family, and I was wondering if there is anything I can do to help in the situation?

Dr. Brown: Yes, perhaps you could help. I feel bad for the family. She had a heart arrest 10 days ago, and at first I didn't think she was going to make it. She's gradually been showing some signs of improvement, but it's been discouraging. Her breathing and heart rate have improved, so she's now off the respirator, but her brain damage is quite bad. Her progress has been poor and slow. When the brain doesn't work well, usually the patient gets an infection in the lungs. She had a tracheotomy the other day.

Pastor Schmidt: I imagine some decisions will have to be made by the family in the near future.

Dr. Brown: Yes, that's true.

Pastor Schmidt: Well, I appreciate your help. Do you think it would be all right to tell the family this information?

Dr. Brown: Yes, that would be fine

Pastor Schmidt: Well, thank you. It's good to get information to the family. They will appreciate it.

Dr. Brown: Good-bye.

Notice that the pastor carefully allowed the physician to express whatever information she thought would be useful to the family, without asking probing questions. Then, the pastor carefully checked with the doctor whether it would be appropriate for him to share information with the family. This is very important. Sometimes the physician will share information that will be especially helpful to the visitor in caring for the patient, but would not be appropriate for the family. Often, the physician will prefer to convey the information to the family in such a way as to sustain or build trust in the physician.

Note, too, that the phone call could just as well have been made by a lay visitor. Had the parish visitor made the call, she could have begun by introducing herself: "This is Mrs. Plath, the pastoral visitor from Trinity Church. I have been visiting the Wilkins family, and I was wondering. . . ." When it does not seem feasible for the parish visitor to make the contact with the doctor, the pastor may do it and then convey the information to the visitor.

The members of the medical staff may welcome your help in translating the often arcane-sounding medical information into simple, everyday language for the family or patient. It is important, therefore, that you ask the doctor for the meaning of every medical phrase or term you do not understand. Patients often are uneasy about doing this. Perhaps they do not want to seem to be biting the hand that heals them. Doctors are busy, and often, because of the great amount of their medical and scientific training, they have not had the time to have necessary additional training in human relations—what used to be called "bedside manner." Thus they themselves often feel uncomfortable in visiting with the patient beyond the technical and professional level. They may cover this by appearing not to have time to talk with patients. The patient may feel, not always justly, that the doctor does not want to talk with them. Therefore, the physician may often appreciate your help at this level. If you do not understand the medical language, feel free also to consult nurses and other members of the staff so that you can more effectively communicate with the patient.

5

Prayer with the Sick

"I'm Richard Klein from the chaplain's office. I stopped in to see how you are feeling."

"Oh, thank you so much, we surely need some support."

It was the grandmother who responded. She and the mother of a two-year-old baby were seated beside a crib.

"Viola here has been here all night, and we're pretty upset." The grandmother went on, "They say Julie's condition is stabilized, whatever that means."

"That usually means leveled off, holding her own," the visitor explained.

"That's good," said the grandmother with a sigh of relief. Then she looked up at the visitor and asked, "Would you say a prayer for us and Julie?"

Praying isn't always easy. In our culture it is almost easier to talk about other intimate areas of life than about our prayer life. The request, "Will you pray for me?" can often be revealing and personal. We sense this in ourselves and in others, so we hesitate to bring up the matter. However, it is helpful to remember that being ill, particularly suddenly ill and hospitalized, is a crisis, and the person we are visiting may especially appreciate our attention to his or her "spiritual life." Prayer as a cry for support and help will often be especially helpful and appreciated.

When to pray

When should we pray with a patient? The first and most obvious answer to that question is: when the patient asks. Quite simple, yet also complex. Sometimes the request that we pray *for* another arises out of a notion that the person making the request is not able to pray properly. The sickroom may not be the place to deal with this notion, but if we sense that the patient feels this way, our manner of praying may be altered in such a way as not to foster these ideas, but to modify them. We should always be careful not to leave the impression that we are eager to take over the responsibility and opportunity of prayer life for others. Dispelling this notion is one important reason for lay persons to become involved alongside the pastor in various tasks of pastoral care, such as visiting the sick.

Another aspect of this notion of praying *for* someone else is the not uncommon idea that the visitor's prayers will be more effective than the prayers of the sufferer: "After all, I'm just an ordinary person . . . I don't even get to church very often, why should God listen to my prayers? You are a good Christian, God will surely listen to your prayers before he'll listen to me!" Some people even think that a special kind of language is necessary for prayer to be heard.

When the patient asks, "Will you pray for me?" the visitor should respond in a way that enhances the possibility the patient will also begin to dialog with God. The visitor should make it clear that God hears the prayers of all who come to him. It is well to pray in a way that will model how anyone might pray to our heavenly Father.

The decision as to whether or not to pray becomes more difficult if there is no request for prayer, and the visitor is uncertain about how prayer might be received, or if it is even meaningful for the patient. In a general way it is useful for the visitor to consider how he or she is being perceived. If the visitor is seen as a representative of the people of God and is visiting a member of the congregation, then it generally can be assumed that prayer is both anticipated and appropriate (unless there are clear and obvious counterindications such as noise, interruptions by staff or visitors, or lack of privacy). Prayer with the sick person is part of the congregation's intercessory prayer, which the visitor personalizes by his or her own presence.

Further indications that prayer would be welcomed and appropriate comes from careful listening to the tone of the entire conversation with the patient. The following excerpt will demonstate what I mean. The visitor is talking with a middle-aged woman who is waiting at the bedside of her comatose husband.

Visitor: How long has John been in the hospital?
Wife: It's been a week or so, and each time it gets worse for him and for the children. I have three daughters. They do all they can to help us.
Visitor: That certainly does make it hard on you, doesn't it?

Wife: No, not really. It is frustrating to see him like this, but that is part of life. I already put my order in with God and told him how I would like to die. I told him I did not want to die of a stroke or suffer. I want to have a heart attack and get it over with. Have you ever asked God for those sorts of things?
Visitor: No, not yet.

Prayer would surely have been appropriate in this visit, because the person being visited—the wife of the sick patient—was using what is sometimes called "ultimate language," expressions of concern about the big issues in life: illness, death, the providence of God. Another form of this is "church talk," or as some have called it, "God talk." This may include conversation about affairs of the congregation, expressions of apology for not being able to go to church, inquiries about the pastor or other members of the congregation, or expressions of appreciation for hymns, psalms, or other portions of Scripture. Often the patient may be using this language to give a signal that he or she wants to deal with what we often call "spiritual issues," both in conversation and in prayer. Usually, therefore, whenever a person is expressing ultimate concerns or talking about church life, this should be taken as an indication that prayer is appropriate and meaningful.

There is one more clear occasion for prayers. That is for intercessory prayer before the visit. I have already indicated that a brief prayer for sensitivity, openness to the Spirit's leading, and compassion for the one about to be visited is an important preparation for every visit. But intercessory prayer for the patient is also important at other times; it could be a part of the public worship of the entire congregation and a part of the visitor's personal prayer life. Intercessory prayer should not be thought of as lobbying God on behalf of our friend, but rather, through this work of compassion, helping us become more fully a part of God's care for the one who is sick or suffering. By interceding for another we are taking that person's side, but we are also standing with God in his care for the one who is ill.

There are times when it is appropriate not to pray in our visits. That may seem strange. Isn't prayer always in order? Intercessory prayer, yes. But we who live with a trust in God's grace must also be cautious about imposing our faith on others. Prayer may not always be appropriate if the patient rejects the message of God's grace or is ignorant about the meaning of prayer and does not desire it. Prayer is dialog with God, a living conversation. It is not a magic incantation to be said over someone to induce a miracle of some sort. Prayer should never be used either to manipulate God or to manipulate or overwhelm another person. The visitor will need to be sensitive in the use of prayer with someone about whose faith-life he or she knows little. Often, especially in the hospital, the call will come to visit persons who are friends of members of the congregation . . . or others about whom the congregation is concerned, but who are not believers themselves. Approaching prayer with this sort of person will need to be done sensitively. Prayer also ought never be used as an evangelistic technique. But let me emphasize again, for these persons, as for everyone, private intercessory prayer is always appropriate.

Prayer, especially in the hospital room, is often awkward or embarrassing when there is not sufficient privacy to allow for quiet concentration and reflection on what one is praying about and to whom one is praying. Therefore, in some situations in which prayer should normally be appropriate, the visitor may have to choose not to pray. Prayer is an intimate dialog and calls for the baring of one's soul and spirit to God and to others who are sharing the prayer; it is insensitive and sometimes even harmful, to ignore the importance of appropriate conditions for prayer.

The sensitive pastoral visitor needs to give careful thought to determining whether the need for prayer is his or her own need or the need of the person being visited. If the visitor is *compassionately* sharing with the patient (or other family member), it will be that person's prayer need that is addressed.

What to pray

It is not unusual for a pastor to encounter people who say, "I don't know how to pray. You pray for me." Often this indicates a notion that a special language is needed in order to guarantee that prayers will be heard. This is not surprising, considering that most of the prayers we hear are framed in the liturgical language of public worship. The language of personal prayer is simply the language of human longing and face-to-face conversation. This is beautifully shown by our Lord, who, in response to the disciples' request "Lord, teach us to pray," said simply, "When you pray, say, 'Father' " (Luke 11:1-2). He did not use the grand language of temple worship: "Lord God, King of the Universe!" So it is important that we develop the facility for speaking to God, on behalf of others, in the simple language of a child making a request of a beloved father. Our language will be of great help in modeling prayer for others who may be uncertain about praying their own prayers.

What to pray for again depends on careful listening during the entire conversation. The Prayer of the Day in public worship used to be called the Collect, because the central theme of the worship was collected into one concise prayer. Many of the Prayers of the Day we now use are classic collects that have been handed down through the church for centuries. This model of the Collect, the gathering together of the themes of central concern, is a good one to use in prayer with the sick. When the visitor is asked to pray for someone, he or she is being asked to collect that person's concerns and bring them before the throne of mercy. The visitor's prayer should gather up only the central themes of concern that have been expressed by the sick person. The ideal prayer, in my judgment, is one in which the content— the words of thanksgiving and the pleas for help—is shared by visitor and patient. It is one that the patient or the parishioner would immediately recognize as his or her own prayer, even though it is being voiced by the visitor.

There are also some dangers in praying. It is important to remember the direction of prayer. Sometimes we are tempted to use prayer as a back-handed way of getting a point across to the person we are visiting—a point that we could not express during the normal conversation. Once, as a chaplain, I was praying with the mother of a six-year-old boy who was dying of leukemia. The mother had been told the diagnosis, but she had been trying desperately to sweep it out of her mind, to deny it. As a consequence, we were not able to talk together about her boy's impending death. I thought I was being careful to avoid trying to get a point across through prayer, but at the end of the prayer, the mother looked up at me and said, "You think he's going to die, don't you?" She had caught me. It opened up more conversation, but it was, nevertheless, a misuse of prayer. Prayer is not a lecture to the person we are visiting; it is our collection of that person's expressed concerns brought before God.

Sometimes when we are asked to pray, it may be helpful to respond with, "What would you like us to pray for?" This might open up some sharing of what special prayer concerns should be addressed to God. It might also help the person to focus more sharply on special understandings that may have developed in the course of the visit. Whenever the visitor asks a question like this, he or she should be sure the patient understands why it is being asked and will be able to give an answer.

It is not unusual, though I do not recommend it as a regular practice, to ask the patient, "Would you like me to pray *with* you?" (rather than "*for* you"). But here again, it is always wiser to ask this only when the visitor is already quite sure what the answer will be. This avoids embarrassing or manipulating the person, and avoids also the visitor's embarrassment. Such a question may also help to focus the entire conversation on life under God, or it may help the visit focus more on the One who is our refuge and strength, especially in times of trouble. A question like this, however, should never be used as a subtle way of saying, "The visit is over."

Too often prayer become the visitor's doorknob—a way to get out, so that "Amen" is often the last word spoken in a pastoral visit. This is also a misuse of prayer. Prayer ought to be the high point, the climax of a visit, not its conclusion. To achieve this, the visitor can place prayer more or less in the final third of the visit, allowing some time at the close of the prayer for further conversation or reflection. The patient will not always seize the opportunity, but it should be offered.

If we have been listening carefully and are serious about our task of collecting the prayer concerns of the person we are visiting, our prayer will be specific. It will be a prayer that fits only that person, not a ready-to-wear prayer that anyone could put on. It will also be voiced in the language familiar to the patient. Such prayer takes practice, as well as sensitive listening and ready compassion.

6

The Use of Scripture in Visiting

As he entered the room, the parish visitor noted a large-print Bible lying on the bed of the woman whom he had come to see. Mrs. Fabricius had suffered a stroke that paralyzed her left side, but she was now at least no longer at death's door.

Visitor: When I visited with you the last time, you were very much concerned about your husband and daughter. How are they doing?

Mrs. Fabricius: They're doing fine. I want to thank you for visiting my husband.

Visitor: We're all concerned about your family, as well as about you. Sometimes being in the hospital is as hard on them as it is on you.

Mrs. Fabricius: Yes, that's true. I am grateful.

Visitor: I see you have a Bible lying on your bed. You told me of your love for the Lord when I visited you before. Are you able to read?

Mrs. Fabricius: My daughter reads for me when she is here.

Visitor: You enjoy that. Would you like for me to read
a while to you now?

After reading some marked passages out of her Bible,
the visitor asked: "Would you like to join in praying the
Lord's Prayer?" Her eyes sparkled an obvious yes. After
praying, the visitor then placed his hand on her forehead
and blessed her: "May God bless and keep you. May he
make his face shine on you. May he lift his countenance
upon you and give you peace. Amen."

This visit demonstrates several important things both
about a pastoral visit and about the use of Scripture in
visiting. First of all, it's a typical visit one would make to
a faithful member of the congregation. Among persons
of this sort and also of the generation from which Mrs.
Fabricius comes, both Scripture reading and prayer
would be common practice. In a sense what happened
here simply continued, in the strange environment of
the hospital, her daily devotional pattern. Where there
is such a pattern, it should certainly be preserved, if at
all possible. Many regular participants in worship make
use of daily devotional booklets like *Christ in Our Home,*
and *The Upper Room,* made available by church publishing houses. The visitor was alert to this pattern of daily
devotion when he noted her large-print Bible lying on
the bed. It is important to be alert for cues of this sort
which provide real direction for ministry.

It is important to note, too, that the visitor properly
read passages from Scripture that were familiar to the
patient. This is especially important in the crisis of serious illness. Under the stress of crisis, a person often
has difficulty marshalling energy to appreciate properly

the puzzling or difficult-to-understand passages of Scripture. It is much more helpful to reflect on words of promise and comfort that are well-known. For some persons this will awaken memorized passages that can be reflected on after the visit is over; this has the effect of prolonging the personal contact and strength of the visit. One should be cautious, however, not to overuse passages such as Psalm 23 or John 14, which may have been wrung dry of meaning through mindless repetition.

Later, if a patient becomes stronger, the use of Scripture might be expanded. The same passages, or at least some of them, might be read again, and in addition, the visitor can encourage the patient to say a bit about what each of these passages have meant for him or her in the past and what promise and hope they provide now. In such reflective conversation, the Word of God comes alive much more vividly than when it is just read.

As with prayer, the strong temptation with reading Scripture is to use it as the way to end the visit. This is a misuse of Scripture. The words of the Bible are not what makes the visit "religious" or "pastoral"; neither are the words of the Bible a talisman that magically bring blessing to whoever says them. Entering into reflective dialog about what has been read will do much to overcome this misunderstanding. To make this possible, the visit should be planned so that the reading and reflecting on Scripture can come during the last half, but not as the last word.

Usually prayer and Scripture go together. They need not, however. Prayer may come before the use of scripture passages, as well as after. Some care should be given that the scripture passages reflect or reinforce the themes of the prayers, particularly if the visitor has been effective in collecting the prayer concerns of the patient.

One need not feel compelled always to use Scripture *and* prayer in a visit. Either can be helpful alone. Sometimes it is most helpful to use Scripture by itself, without a prayer, particularly where the scripture passage is already a form of prayer, as with the Psalms. And certainly one can pray in a visit without also reading or reciting some words of Scripture.

In reading Scripture to persons, avoid the temptation to read the familiar verses without expression. Holy language is not sanctified by a monotone. Scripture should be read like a letter from a dear friend. This is in fact what the visitor is doing—sharing a message from God, addressed to the patient. The visitor is the messenger and should strive to be as vital and articulate a messenger as possible. The volume of reading and speaking should also be regulated carefully to meet the needs of the patient. This may mean reading more slowly and loudly for older persons who are beginning to experience minor hearing loss. For those who cannot hear at all, the visitor may write out the verses in the patient's presence. This can be much more personal than handing the patient a Bible or Testament to read, and the written portions often are kept at the bedside for later reference. If the patient has a small tape recorder which he or she can easily operate, brief passages can be read on a cassette, perhaps interspersed with music or congregational singing as an extension of the personal visit. Visitors need to use consecrated imagination.

Scripture does not always have to be read in portions from the Bible. Perhaps the most effective use of Scripture is if it seasons the language of the visitor. By this I do not mean simply the rote recital of memorized passages (though that is often very useful), but interspersing one's speech with images and analogies from God's

Word. The use of analogy can be especially helpful in relating the situation or feelings of the patient to those of a biblical character.

Consider this visit: A middle-aged man is explaining about a dream.

Patient: You know, I saw Jesus Christ in a dream. I was heading in the wrong direction with my life, and he was telling me so in my dream. I had broken up a family and a home.
Visitor: What do you think you could do about the situation as you see it now?
Patient: I really loved my wife. I have loved her all these years and I am sorry that I hurt her so very much for so long. I think I will telephone her and speak with her as soon as I can.

At this point the visitor might respond with something like this: "Right now you feel a bit like the prodigal son in Jesus' parable, who finally came to his senses and realized what he had been doing with his life and wanted very much to let his father know that he felt bad."

Often people are hesitant about expressing their grief and sorrow over some loss, and the judicious use of the language of the Psalms may help them give voice to their grieving. Such imagery and helpful expression of sorrow we find in Psalm 31:

Be gracious to me, O Lord, for I am in distress;
my eye is wasted from grief,
my soul and my body also.
For my life is spent with sorrow,

and my heart with sighing;
my strength fails because of my misery,
and my bones waste away (vv. 9-11).

What Scripture should one use?

Scripture is such a vast treasure! How shall one select what passages to use in visiting the sick? First of all, it is well to be guided by the same principle that has been suggested with respect to prayer: respond to the expressed need of the patient. Sometimes the needs are not openly expressed, only hinted at; at other times, they are clear and obvious. This requires, however, that the visitor be quite familiar with Scripture and, ideally, have much of Scripture committed to memory. The memorizing of scripture passages that seemed like a burdensome assignment in church school or confirmation instruction is then rewarded. To facilitate this familiarity with Scripture, my suggestion to students in seminary classes is always that they build for themselves a pastoral-care notebook that can easily be carried in pocket or purse. In the notebook students list scripture passages under various headings of need. It is also helpful to keep a listing of passages that have been shared with people, with a brief note about the occasion. For the beginning of this collection of passages, a suggestion is given at the close of this chapter.

A special resource in pastoral care is the Psalms, the prayerbook of God's people. Special familiarity with the Psalms is important, for they speak to all the situations of life and hold up again and again the central theme of the steadfast love and compassion of God.

Some attention should be given to making sure that the language of Scripture fits the taste as well as the needs of the patient, both as regards his or her under-standing as well as what may contribute to his or her sense of the transcendent. In our spiritual work with the sick we want to express not only the knowledge that God is deeply with us in our suffering and pain, but also our gratitude to God and our joy that God is not bound by our humanness, that God continues to offer strength, vision, and hope. This is often most clearly expressed in Scripture. As a pastor, I have had the experience of read-ing some passages of Scripture to people in their mother tongue. Often it was a language no longer used in daily discourse, but in a time of crisis, reading passages from Scripture in that language was a powerful symbol of the never-ending care of God. The visitor must give careful consideration to the age of the patient in selecting pas-sages and in selecting the language or translation in which Scripture is read.

One frequently has to infer the needs of the sick per-son to which Scripture can speak. A patient will rarely say, for example, "I need hope." Instead, the patient may express a sense of hopelessness. The visitor has to listen between the words, as it were, to pick up that the patient may be grieving or may need to grieve, or that the patient is afraid. The exercise of compassion coupled with fa-miliarity with the rich resources of Scripture are the vis-itor's best guides in doing this.

In regular visits with people who are home-bound, or others who may not be seriously ill, or who have not voiced a particular spiritual need, a most helpful re-source is the lectionary, the lessons read in the weekly worship of the congregation. Reading these, and per-haps leaving the bulletin or insert on which they are printed, with persons who are shut off from the com-munity's faith life is an excellent way of including them.

It is remarkable, too, how often these lessons do speak directly to the situation of the patient.

It should be readily obvious that not all passages of Scripture are of equal value in the care of the sick. Through their use in the church, some passages have taken on a symbolic meaning beyond their actual content. Imagine for a moment that you are a middle-aged person just admitted to the hospital with a heart attack; the diagnosis is not yet clear and no one seems to know for certain how serious it is. A parish visitor comes to see you, and in the course of the visit reads to you John 14 or Psalm 23. What are you likely to think? Quite naturally, that you are dying. The fright that this may give you might even make your physical situation worse. The passages chosen communicated this additional message because most of us have heard them frequently as a part of the funeral service, so we associate them with death.

Prescriptive use of Scripture

Another way of using Scripture was suggested several years ago by one of the early pioneers in the pastoral care movement, John S. Bonnell. When he felt the occasion appropriate, he would give a person he was caring for a short Bible passage that seemed to speak especially to his or her situation, much like a physician prescribes a medicine to meet a special need, rather than just giving aspirin for everything. Such a passage becomes a personal source of strength when hope fades, pain becomes severe, or fear threatens to take over. Current findings on the importance of meditation, concentrated reflecting on a central theme, bear out the helpfulness of this approach.

Let me voice two cautions, however. One is against the moralistic use of passages in this prescriptive sense. We may be tempted to use passages to make people experience the feelings we think they ought to have, or to renounce feelings that they actually do have. Compassionate judgment can protect against this temptation. On the other hand, there is also the danger that passages used in this way take on a talismanic character, like a good-luck charm which magically wards off danger, or guarantees healing or help in the terms desired by the patient. We need to remember that God is not a magician. Our careful selection of passages can guard against this danger.

Religious literature

The use of tracts or religious literature is a matter that requires careful judgment, particularly when visiting people in the hospital. Every nurse and hospital chaplain can tell horror stories of scurrilous tracts that have been indiscriminately passed around and that have generally given the church a bad reputation in hospitals. I have seen lying on hospital bed pillows tracts entitled, "Are You Prepared to Die?" left by misguided persons who thought they were doing the Lord's work. In my judgment a religious leaflet or tract should *never* be left anonymously on someone's bed or bedside table; that is just about as effective as spreading the gospel by flying an airplane over the land and dropping pages of the Bible. The visitor should always personally hand the tract or religious leaflet to the recipient. In this way, literature is received *within* a personal relationship and can be regarded as an extension of personal concern. A number of suitable booklets of prayers and scripture passages are available from Augsburg Publishing House and other church publishers. These can be most helpful, but they should be given as a part of the personal visit and dialog with the patient, never as a substitute for it.

The Scriptures are one of the most valuable resources for our faith and life, and are particularly valued during the crisis time of illness. The importance of Scripture in the care of the sick, however, is not automatic; the words of the Bible are not a magic charm, but are the clear word and promise of God, "I will never fail you or forsake you." Hence we can confidently say, "The Lord is my helper, I will not be afraid" (Heb. 13:5-6). For the sensitive, compassionate parish visitor the words and promises of God are an invaluable resource in bringing comfort and the blessing of God.

7

Worship Resources for Visiting

We have particularly rich resources for ministry to the sick in the liturgical materials available to us in the church. Worship rites often convey what conversation cannot. The dependable and familiar words and prayers and the ritual actions provide channels for the expression of our deepest emotions and highest hopes. Especially in times of illness and other crises, the durability and enduring nature of these rites bring comfort and serve to contain the wild fears that threaten to overcome us.

The ministry of a thoughtful, compassionate visitor of the sick will be vastly enriched by these resources, available in all Christian churches. Some churches have a more elaborately developed liturgical tradition than others, but all Christian churches share in two sacraments, Baptism and Holy Communion. All churches also share in the classic prayers of Christendom, and most share the common creeds. In addition, many denominations have developed services of healing, rites for the blessing of the sick, and prayer resources for the time of dying, the moment of death, and the occasion of burial. Their effective use brings great strength and comfort in times of critical need.

We have already spoken of the use of prayer and Scripture in the care of the sick. In addition, Holy Communion is often offered. The sacrament of the Lord's Supper is called by various names: the Last Supper, Eucharist, the sacramental meal, Holy Communion.

The familial nature of the sacrament of Holy Communion is clear, especially in the writings of St. Paul, who stressed its communal nature:

> The cup of blessing which we bless, is it not a participation in the blood of Christ? The bread which we break, is it not a participation in the body of Christ? Because there is one bread, we who are many are one body, for we all partake of the one bread (1 Cor. 10:16-18).

From its inception, this meal was given to the disciples as an expression of their corporate fellowship with Jesus as Lord. The sacrament is not a blessing provided simply for the edification of our private spiritual life. Yet the blessings the sacrament offers us as members of the fellowship of believers are personal. As Luther puts it in the Small Catechism: "In the sacrament we receive forgiveness of sins, life and salvation." Through the gifts of bread and wine in which Christ's body and blood, his very person are given, he enters into communion with us, draws us into communion with himself, and bonds us into communion with each other in the family of faith. For those who are isolated by illness and suffering, this understanding of Communion can mean a great deal. It can "sacramentalize," make vivid and alive through actions of eating and drinking, that they are not abandoned by Christ nor by his family, the church. Therefore, it is important to emphasize the family nature of this sacramental meal.

This is done in two ways: first, through the distribution of the elements of bread and wine to those who are by virtue of illness temporarily separated from the worshiping community. The same elements that are used in the congregational celebration of the meal are taken from the altar and distributed to the scattered members of the family as a way of signifying that they, too, belong to the gathered family. Secondly, as a member from the congregation, the pastoral visitor is the bearer of the gifts of Christ given to his church, to be shared by all members of that church. The visitor carries the meal as an emissary, a servant of the congregation to whom Christ has given these gifts. Since the elements of bread and wine have been consecrated by the presiding minister in the public worship, there is no need to further consecrate them when they are carried to the bedside or sickroom of isolated members of the congregation.

Celebration of Holy Communion with the sick

In every way possible, the visitor should indicate that the reception of the sacrament in the sickroom or at the retirement center or health care center is an extension of the congregational celebration. A bit of attention to the setting of the bedside table, decked with a clean napkin from which as much as possible of the hospital or medical paraphernalia have been removed, with perhaps a small set of candles and cross modeled after those in the sanctuary, are all helpful. Helpful, too, is the judicious use of taped congregational singing, especially of the communion hymns. Keep in mind that it is often difficult for sick persons to sustain attention for a longer period of time, especially when they cannot participate in some way. Sharing the bulletin of the day, copies of the lessons and the prayer of the day are additional helps in including the isolated sick person into the worship life of the congregation.

Further suggestions and many helpful directions for sharing the Holy Communion with the sick are provided in the helpful booklet by Philip H. Pfatteicher, *Distributing Communion to the Sick and Homebound,* published by Augsburg Publishing House and Fortress Press. Though written particularly for Lutherans, it also has helpful suggestions for those of other denominations.

There will be some denominational variations in the manner of distribution or celebration of Communion with the sick and homebound. Some denominations, including Roman Catholic, most Reformed churches, and some Lutherans, permit only the pastor to either consecrate or serve the elements. Others, such as the Episcopal, most Lutheran, and some of the Methodist churches, permit lay distribution of the consecrated elements, as we have described it here. It will be important, therefore, for the congregational lay visitor to confer with the pastor as to what is appropriate. The sacramental ministry, particularly, should always be carried on only under the close and careful supervision of the ordained parish pastor, who by New Testament tradition is to preside over this ministry. Therefore, the careful parish visitor will never undertake this ministry without such supervision.

In the case of the homebound or the chronically ill person who is isolated from the congregational life for long months or years, it is advisable to depart from the practice of distributing the elements consecrated at the congregational altar. Because of the extended isolation from congregational worship life, it is important to provide for the consecration of the bread and wine of the Lord's Supper in the presence of those who are to receive it. Some care should be taken to make clear that this is not a special or different kind of sacramental celebration; it is an opportunity for the person not able to attend church to participate in this worshipful way in the consecration of the elements. Since in most denominations such consecration must be conducted by the ordained pastor, this full celebration requires the presence of the pastor as well as the regular lay visitor. In this way it is possible to symbolize that the unordained parish visitor is an extension of the ministry of the ordained pastor, who is an expression of the church's ministry.

Therefore, it is appropriate for the lay visitor to function as assisting minister in the consecration of the bread and wine, just as lay persons serve as assistant ministers in the sacramental celebration of the congregation. The visitor as assistant can read appropriate scripture lessons and prayers and participate with the sick person in the eating and drinking. Participation by members of the family would also add meaning to the service.

Why not the pastor?

Lay visitors of the sick often encounter the reaction, "Well, I appreciate your visit, but I wish the pastor could have come." It may not be worded in quite that blunt a fashion, but that is the sentiment. There is the feeling that only the pastor is sufficient to speak the words of grace or comfort; anyone else is a weak substitute. We need to recognize that this attitude is normal and arises out of the nature of group life and the function of leaders. It cannot be changed just by a theological explanation. It has to do with the sense of helplessness that the crises of life arouse and the dependency we then feel on a strong leader or rescuer. And generally speaking, the more grave the crisis, the greater the dependency on the strength of a leader.

These attitudes, however, can be changed by a careful review of the biblical understanding of ministry, particularly a New Testament understanding of the nature of pastoral functions. Let it suffice for the moment to point out that the gifts of the Spirit to the churches are gifts to the community of faith, not to individuals in isolation from that community. Furthermore, the functions in this community of faith are varied and complex, so that the apostle Paul used the human body as an analogy to explain the complex interrelatedness of this community (1 Corinthians 12). Furthermore, the gift of power or authority is given to the community, not to individuals, and delegated by the community to individuals who function on behalf of the congregation. It is in this delegated sense that the visitor functions on behalf of the congregation as minister in the special rituals helpful to the sick. The fundamental basis of all ministries in the church is our common Baptism. In Baptism, we are all initiated into the family of God, the ministering community, the church.

For these reasons it is well to avoid a situation in which always the same person visits a particular person who is sick or homebound. Rotation of visitors will demonstrate that the ministry is of the congregation, not simply the particular visitor or the pastor. And when the question is raised, "Is the pastor too busy, so that he sent you?" the visitor may simply explain the nature of shared ministries in the life of the congregation. A word of caution, however: a severe illness-crisis is not the time to do this.

The visitor who functions as the primary or sole minister in the use of these rituals must be trained carefully by the pastor, so that he or she feels secure and comfortable in this role. The greater the sense of self-composure the visitor has, the more secure and comfortable the recipients of that ministry will be. When the visitor and the pastor decide that it is important for the pastor to function as chief ministrant, the visitor should still try to be present to function as assisting minister. This can easily be arranged, as noted above, because in all of the rituals there are occasions for the reading of scripture passages or prayers. When the visitor functions as primary minister, family members or other members of the congregation can become the assistants. Always the fundamental concern should be: "How can we communicate the corporate nature of the life and ministry of the congregation and the importance of the person for whom we are caring, who is temporarily isolated from this corporate life?"

The hand of blessing

Another simple act, that we do almost automatically when caring for others, is touching. This has become a special ritual called the "laying on of hands" (an awkward phrase, but there seems to be no substitute). It need not be confined to a ritualized worship setting, because it is a normal and I hope common experience in visiting the sick. Unless circumstances dictate otherwise, the visitor should always grasp the hand of the sick person when praying. This handclasp conveys the compassion we feel and hope to carry out. A handclasp says that the visitor is sincerely and deeply with the person being visited. We have already noted how important this is for the one who is sick. A handclasp of this sort is one form of laying on of hands.

A hand on the shoulder is another form and is sometimes an advisable substitute for the handclasp, as in the case of someone suffering with severe arthritis of the hands. However, two cautions are in order here: the most obvious one, of course, is that the touch should be genuine—not merely perfunctory. The second caution has to do with eroticism. This is also a matter of genuineness: the personal touch should convey only compassion, nothing more or less. One needs to gauge carefully how touching and handclasping will be received or perceived by the recipient. Will it be perceived as a compassionate handclasp or as holding hands? Will the touch on the shoulder or arm be perceived as a sexual advance?

It may seem strange to be so explicit about this in a book on the spiritual care of the sick, but it is important to consider, because, in the experience of illness, the elemental emotions of both patient and visitor are much closer to the surface. One must, therefore, be especially attentive to the implications of actions that might exploit these fundamental feelings.

The ritual action for the laying on of hands is simply the placing of one or both hands on top of the person's head. If, however, the patient is lying down, then one or both hands might be placed on the person's forehead, or on the shoulder. Common sense and good judgment should dictate which is best. With this laying on of hands, a word of grace or blessing or a prayer is spoken. This might be the Aaronic Blessing, "The Lord bless you and keep you. The Lord make his face shine upon you and be gracious to you. The Lord look upon you with favor

and give you peace." The sign of the cross might conclude the prayer. Whatever prayer or blessing is used, it
would be wise to have it conform to the blessings normally spoken in the regular worship life of the congregation—words that are familiar and bring to mind the
past blessings of God. I would caution against trying to
make this too intimate or personal, at the risk of becoming sentimental or even maudlin and thus trivializing the
blessing of God. This ritual, after all, is intended to convey God's blessing, not ours alone.

In the chapter on the care of the dying, I will mention
one more ritual that can be most useful, the commendation or blessing of the dying. If carefully and thought-
fully ministered, all of these rituals can serve to bring
great comfort and the mighty assurances of Christian
faith and hope to the sick and the members of their
family.

8

Ministry to the Dying

In our culture we go to great lengths to deny the reality of death. Death seems to be the absolute antithesis of life, such a contradiction to vital activity and awareness that we easily accept the notion that somehow it will not come to us. The belief that some Eastern cultures have, that death is a part of living, is foreign to many of us. The South African Zulus have a phrase that I often wish we could capture; they speak of a "ripe death," conveying the idea that as a fruit is ripe for plucking, one is ripe or ready for dying. Wise pastors realize that one may think of the whole ministry to people in terms of "ripening them" for the time of death. Ministry with the sick, particularly those who are diagnosed as terminally ill, may be understood as the art of preparing people for a "ripe death."

Why is it so difficult to talk with each other about dying? Perhaps the first reason is that we have not truly come to terms with dying ourselves, and so it frightens us as much, or even more, than it frightens others. We have to come to terms with what our dying means for us before we can comfortably talk with another about dying. One way of doing this is to imagine that you are on an airliner flying at 38,000 feet, when suddenly the pilot announces that the engines have failed, and a crash is imminent. Imagine the thoughts you might have as you plummet to earth and certain death. This is not a comfortable exercise, but it does help us to gain some perspective on dying. Those who have been ill and close to death themselves may be better equipped than most of us for this difficult ministry.

One of the frequent impediments to being able to share dying with the one who is ill is the conspiracy of silence in which family members and sometimes medical professionals strive to withhold the bad news from the dying person, for fear that he or she will not be able to take it. It is important to know that when a medical diagnosis is terminal, that is, it seems evident that the disease or trauma can only end in death, the physician is bound by professional ethics to inform the next of kin. Sometimes at this point the family pleads with the doctor, "Don't tell dad!" and the pastor and the pastoral visitor may be drawn into the conspiracy. Doctors are increasingly less willing to agree to this, most preferring to inform the patient directly of the nature of the prognosis. This, in most instances, is for the best. The concerned visitor, however, should not go too far in supporting the doctor in this, especially by forcing the patient to speak of death and dying before he or she is ready. The visitor must instead listen carefully to the clues that tell when the patient is ready.

The visitor may be the best help in sustaining and supporting the members of the family so that they can live *with* the tragic news and live *through* that news with the one who is dying. This may involve talking with members of the family about what it means to know that their loved one is dying and helping them to become increasingly comfortable in talking about the death, so that they in turn can share with the patient the meaning of the dying experience.

One of the most significant gifts of compassionate care, then, can be to open up communication between members of the family and the dying person. Such sharing shatters the loneliness that otherwise enshrouds the dying person as others, including members of the hospital staff and the medical profession, avoid intimate personal contact. Many of us fear not dying itself, but dying alone. When my mother was drowned in a mountain flood several years ago, the thought that haunted me most in the year following was not her death, but her death *alone* in a swirling mountain stream. One can also die alone in a modern, stainless-steel hospital with its hustle of staff and attendants. Breaking the conspiracy of silence can help to shatter the loneliness of dying and make incarnate the possibility of dying in the Lord.

As Christians, our best resource in facing death and ministering to a dying person is our resurrection hope that we have in Christ, our risen Savior. As we face death with others, we will fall back on these promises, not as a way of avoiding death but as a way of journeying through it into the mysteries of the fulfillment of the promised new life in Christ. We must always be ready to share the hope that is within us, as those whom we are serving indicate they are ready to hear. As dying persons discover that we are comfortable in dealing with these issues, they may open the way for us to share our own faith. One needs to be careful here not to be argumentative or even persuasive. Rather, the simple sharing of our genuinely held faith, which is informed by biblical promises, will be sufficient.

One of the most helpful aspects for our resurrection faith is the reality that Christ our Lord has himself gone through the pilgrimage of dying. Because of this, his promise that he will never forsake us can bring great comfort and strength even in this darkest hour. The conviction that "neither death, nor life, nor angels, nor principalities, nor things present, nor things to come, nor powers, nor height, nor depth, nor anything else in all creation, will be able to separate us from the love of God in Christ Jesus our Lord" (Rom. 8:38-39) is a great sustaining hope that is ours to share.

Recent studies on death and dying have discovered that dying, like living, is a process. Some sociologists speak of a *death trajectory,* or course of dying, which has several identifiable components. The most noteworthy work has probably been done by Dr. Elisabeth Kübler-Ross. She identifies the components of the dying process as including *denial, anger, bargaining, depression,* and *acceptance.* Occasionally these have been incorrectly understood as stages that everyone goes through in dying. They are simply analytical concepts that help us to understand what many people feel as they face death. Knowing them helps us from being shocked when we observe them. But we should keep in mind that these are not sequential steps that follow one after another in the dying process and not everyone experiences them all. As we listen carefully, we may hear feelings that express several of these processes at the same time, or we may find that a person has moved back and forth between two or more of these components. Usually, however, the person can reach deeper levels of acceptance of death as he or she is helped to work through the

various other components of the pilgrimage through
dying.

Let us look at these concepts and draw some implications for ministry.

Shock and denial

This first component seems to be quite universal, particularly when the reality of death comes suddenly. It is
the recoil from devastating news: "This can't be happening to me!" or, "There must be some mistake!" There
may be the frantic effort to get another diagnosis, then
another and another. Sometimes this is accompanied by
the recourse even to forms of faith healing that are not
a normal part of the religious life of the patient.

It is important to remember that a reaction of shock
to sudden tragic news is perfectly normal and is a pro-
tective, preserving response. The inability to feel the
pain in a sudden injury allows one the strength and ability to obtain proper help. The shock reaction permits
the person to get the emotional and spiritual support he
or she needs to bear the heavy load and to grow in readiness to deal with this new reality.

Denial is the avoidance of the reality that confronts
one. The denial reaction is a natural aftermath of the
shock reaction. However, the denial reaction should not
be permitted to continue too long. Careful judgment is
required to determine how long is long enough. If the
denial process seems to be lingering, it is well to consult
with the pastor, the physician, or mental health specialists to find the most helpful ways to deal with it. The
visitor should recognize evidence of denial, such as a
patient, after having been told the diagnosis, still acts as
if he or she does not know what is wrong. Sometimes

patients will refuse to name the disease which they have been told they have.

Ministry to people experiencing shock and denial reactions consists primarily in offering *presence* and *support*. Physical touching and careful listening can be important. In this way the visitor will not encourage denial, but also will not contradict. Presence and support can make it comfortable for the patient or members of the family to cry and express their anger or grief or fear. Interrupting with rational statements that force the truth to come crashing in goes beyond the bounds of presence and support as expressed in touching and listening.

Anger

Even a three-day bout with the flu can make us angry. How much angrier might we feel at being faced with giving up life itself? Frustration at being unable to fulfill the visions and goals of life can easily give way to anger. Emotions are likely to be highly volatile with rage, resentment, fear, terror, and jealousy filling the spirit. Particularly in younger persons there is a sense of being cheated by the illness, or the world, or even God.

The anger that the person who is struggling with death may feel may well be taken out on those who are near at hand: members of the family, hospital staff, the visitors, even God.

Ministry at this point involves being willing to accept the anger; above all one should avoid saying or even implying, "You shouldn't feel this way." Rather the visitor should be willing to be a whipping post and receive the expressions of anger. It is not easy to listen to someone express anger without becoming angry too; but the visitor must strive to avoid this reaction.

Usually the visitor will find that as the patient *voices* his or her anger, it dissipates. One can see this process in many of the psalms of lament. The despair is exploded so that hope will follow.

It is important to help members of the family understand what is going on and enable them to accept the anger without being personally insulted or hurt. The visitor can affirm the fact that even God is not going to be blown out of heaven at our anger. Some of the psalms of lament (like Psalms 55, 88, or 102) may be helpful here, especially in ministering to members of the family.

Bargaining

All of us are tempted to strike a deal when things are going against us. Often people who are dying will try to cajole, beg, or plead with God or their loved ones to perform some miracle or do something, in return for which the patient may make promises that cannot be kept. The bargaining process often grows out of a feeling of guilt. It is an effort at self-justification or the attempt to earn the blessing of life and health once again. It is a last desperate effort to exert one's power and influence over unkind and impersonal forces that are felt to have caused one's misfortune and that can be manipulated by one's power.

Ministry consists first in understanding the meaning of this process; it is part of the struggle to come to terms with the reality that one hates and wishes desperately could be changed. The visitor should allow time for the patient to work through the bargaining without encouraging it. It is important to provide an atmosphere of forgiveness for the bargaining attempts and be ready to clarify the true nature of the forces that seem to be intent on destroying the patient. It may help to talk with the patient about the nature of loving family care and the nature of God's providential care. It is important, also, to help members of the family avoid being caught up in the bargaining process: "I'll leave everything to you in my will, if you will just take me to that clinic" (or "that faith healer"). Also, it is important to prevent the congregation from entering into the bargaining attempts system: "I'll donate money for a new organ, Lord, if you will just make me well again." To comply with promises like that borders on the unethical in ministering to the sick. In the bargaining process, the patient feels much like the victim. That feeling of being victimized should never be exploited.

Depression

Depression is another natural response to the tragic reality that one has to surrender life. Frequent crying, loss of appetite, and difficulty in sleeping are symptoms of depression that may themselves cause even further complications in the illness. Depression is usually a signal that the reality of what is happening is finally and fully perceived. There is often an intense sense of loneliness and self-pity, as though no one else can truly understand the depths of the person's suffering; the person feels much like the psalmist who wrote:

> My heart is in anguish within me,
> the terrors of death have fallen upon me.
> Fear and trembling come upon me,
> and horror overwhelms me (Ps. 55:4-5)

Often during this period, the person may prefer to be alone for longer periods of time, as though already anticipating the loneliness of dying.

Ministry at this point involves a quiet and steady presence. Spiritual comfort and a firm conviction of the love and presence of God are important but should be conveyed without a great deal of talk. The visitor can also help sustain family members and encourage them to see it through to the end. If the person is willing to talk, a process of life review, reflecting on the fulfillments and accomplishments of life may be helpful. This should, however, be carefully done in such a way as to avoid implying that the depressed person shouldn't be depressed. The hope is that through the faithful support of family, friends, lay visitor ministry and ministry of the pastor, the dying person may be able to share the psalmist's conviction:

> Cast your burden on the Lord,
> and he will sustain you; he will never permit
> the righteous to be moved (Ps. 55:22).

Acceptance

Acceptance is the attitude of finally coming to terms with the impending death, accepting it as a final outcome of life. The dying person is now fully able to be reconciled with the loss of the past and the giving up of loving relationships, and has more or less resolved the issues of what will become of those who are left behind. During this time, also, the dying person may prefer solitude or may wish to slow down the pace of personal relationships, perhaps even to the point of not wishing to see anyone except those who are very close. The patient has little energy now for establishing or maintaining new personal relationships. It is at this time that the person has noticeably given up the battle and may physically begin to fade away.

Ministry now is primarily a ministry of presence. Talking may be impossible, but presence is essential. Personal contact through touching may be especially important. Though the dying person may not be able to respond by talking, it is helpful to remember that the sense of hearing lingers on beyond most of the other senses. Even in coma, persons have been known to hear and understand what is being said. Well-known prayers like the Lord's Prayer, or memorized portions of Scriptures are especially significant at this time. Pastoral visits should be short and more frequent.

When patients cannot communicate

Mrs. Meyer suffered a cardiac arrest 10 days ago. She is being faithfully attended in the hospital by her husband and her children. She was on the respirator for a while, because the cardiac arrest had resulted in brain damage. Now she is off the respirator; a tracheotomy has been performed to assist her breathing. She lies comatose in her bed, unable to respond in any way as the parish visitor sees her. Her husband meets the visitor in the hall outside her room.

Husband: They've got her off the respirator. I went in yesterday and rubbed her arm like this *(he demonstrates),* and I could feel a quiver up her arm, kind of like she felt me. She opened her eyes for a second or two.

Visitor: So, she seemed to respond.

Husband: Seemed that way. I'm waiting to find out the latest reports from the doctor. *(The nurse comes out of the room.)* I think they might be done with Sarah now.

The two walk into the room. Lawrence goes right to the bedside where Sarah is lying on her side. She is breathing normally and seems asleep. Her mouth looks crooked and her tongue is limp against her lower lip. A tracheotomy tube is connected to her windpipe. Lawrence touches Sarah, holding her hand. His actions indicate love for her; he lovingly brushes back her hair with his hands. There is little talking during this time. After a time, the visitor speaks to Sarah: "Hello, Sarah. We've come to visit you. Your husband Lawrence is here, and I am Mr. Swenson from Zion Church. We love you, Sarah, and care for you. I would like to say a prayer with you." The visitor takes her hand and prays, "Heavenly Father, we are mindful of your presence here today. We thank you that you are a God who cares very much for us, a God who loves us. Guide the hands of the doctors and nurses, and may they be your instruments of healing. Keep Sarah in your tender, loving arms and let her know that you are near." As the visitor begins the Lord's Prayer, Lawrence, the husband, joins in.

Following the prayer, the visitor places his hand on Sarah's forehead and says the blessing: "The Lord bless you, and keep you. The Lord make his face shine upon you and be gracious unto you. The Lord lift up his countenance upon you, and give you peace. Amen." The older form of the benediction is deliberately used, since it is familiar to Sarah.

Often in ministering to dying patients, the visitor will be in a situation like this one, where the patient is not able to respond verbally in any way. How can the visitor conduct ministry without dialog? The parish visitor here, whose actual account of the visit has been reported in some detail, was very effective in this difficult ministry. Several things are noteworthy about the visit reported above. First, the attention given to the husband and the observation of his relationship to Sarah. Furthermore, the visitor was comfortable in silence. It is important to remember that our composure is just as contagious as our tension. Just by being calm at the bedside, the visitor can bring peace in a time of great stress or pain. Note, too, the use of physical contact, both by Lawrence the husband and also by the visitor. Human touch is a language we too frequently neglect. Finally, observe that the visitor addressed Sarah, speaking simply and with the assumption that she could hear, even though she could not respond. Finally, the laying on of hands in the form of the blessing and using the language of blessing that Sarah would have been familiar with, was an important conveyance of the presence and the peace of God.

In situations in which normal communication seems impossible, the visitor should make use of other resources: calm quietness, loving touch, simple words, proclaiming the presence and peace of God, and finally, the hand of blessing.

In the hour of death

Unfortunately, the hour of death does not always follow the romanticized picture of the extended family gathered in a circle around the bedside, where one by one each member draws close and says a last farewell. Most people now die in the modern hospital unit of a rest home, where there is often a flurry of medical excitement, a plethora of medical equipment, and a climate of frantic crisis. Hardly a situation in which one can pause for worship! It is important, therefore, that the pastor and the parish visitor be innovative and able to improvise with the rites they perform.

The church has provided liturgical resources for the moment of death that can be very meaningful both to the dying person and to the members of the family who are present. In the Roman Catholic church, this is the time for extreme unction or the performance of last rites. Other denominations have their own services for the commendation of the dying. Though it is most likely that the ordained pastor will be present at the time of death and will preside at this ritual, it is appropriate that the lay pastoral visitor also be present, particularly when a long-term relationship has developed over many visits. The lay visitor might well participate in the brief service by reading the Psalms or other scripture passages.

The brief ritual begins with the prayer:

Almighty God, look on _____(name)_____ , whom you made your child in Baptism, and comfort *him/her* with the promise of life with all your saints in your eternal kingdom, the promise made sure by the death and ressurrection of your Son, Jesus Christ our Lord. Amen.

This is followed by an appropriate scripture passage or two. Possibly one of the Psalms that has been used in previous visits with the person would be most fitting. Litanies are provided in the order, which may also be used. Following the litany is the prayer of commendation, at which time the minister says:

God of compassion and love, you have breathed into us the breath of life and have given us the exercise of our minds and wills. In our frailty we surrender all life to you from whom it came, trusting in your gracious promises; through Jesus Christ our Lord.

I would strongly recommend that if at all possible, during this prayer, the minister or lay visitor place the hand of blessing on the forehead of the person, or perhaps hold the hand of the patient.

This prayer is then followed by the Nunc Dimittis:

Lord, now you let your servant go in peace; your word has been fulfilled. My own eyes have seen the salvation which you have prepared in the sight of every people; a light to reveal you to the nations and the glory of your people Israel.

Another blessing could be used:

Depart in peace, you ransomed soul. May God the Father Almighty who created you, Jesus Christ, the Son of the Living God who redeemed you, the Holy Spirit who sanctified you, preserve your going out and your coming in from this time forth, even for evermore. Amen.

Withdrawal of life-support systems

The ritual indicated above can also be used at the time of the withdrawal of life-support systems. The removal of life-support systems is normally done by members of the hospital staff or the medical profession. Following this removal, the minister may say the following prayer:

Into your hands, O merciful Savior, we commend your servant, _____(name)_____ . Acknowledge, we humbly beseech you, a sheep of your own fold, a lamb of your own flock, a sinner of your own redeeming. Receive *him/her* into the arms of your mercy, into the blessed rest of everlasting peace, and into the glorious company of the saints in light.

It is important to bear in mind that all the elements in this order are optional. It may well be that the visitor, the pastor, or a member of the family, may feel moved to write an especially appropriate prayer that can be used.

Ministry to the family at the time of death

Though attention is focused on the dying person, it is important that one not neglect the family members who have suffered alongside the patient for perhaps many months. They have been on the emotional rollercoaster of new hope and dreary despair. The worship resources available also contain a rite for use with the family at the time of death. This rite embraces a psalm appropriate for the situation and other lessons from scripture; here again it would be wise to choose a passage that had been used with the deceased person or was even a favorite passage. Though the pastor might preside at the service, it would be significant if the parish visitor who has been involved in ministry with the deceased and the family were to read appropriate words of Scripture. The rite may conclude with various prayers chosen for the occasion, such as this one:

Almighty God, source of all mercy and giver of comfort: Deal graciously, we pray, with those who mourn, that, casting all their sorrow on you, they may know the consolation of your love; through your Son, Jesus Christ, our Lord. Amen.

The formalities of a prayer must on no account curb the flow of the feelings of pain, loss, anguish, anger, and guilt that flood the consciousness of those who remain. It is appropriate, therefore, that the service include opportunity for the family members to reflect on the life of the deceased. In this informal conversation people should be able to weep and give voice to the highly mixed emotions that they are experiencing. Help family members to avoid the notion that it is somehow a denial of Christian faith to feel sorrow, anguish, anger, and guilt at the death of a loved one. Many of the Psalms provide us with a most helpful model. The following is just one sample of many:

> I cry with my voice to the Lord,
> with my voice I make supplication to the Lord.
> I pour out my complaint before him,
> I tell my trouble before him.
> When my spirit is faint,
> thou knowest the way (Ps. 142:1-2).

It would be helpful to read such a psalm with the family members as they express their grief. God is not just the God of the blessed and the cheerful, but the refuge for those who mourn.

Ministry to the family of a deceased person should not end with the rituals at the sick bed or the funeral home or the funeral itself, but should continue for many months after the loss. The process of grief work requires pastoral care, in which the lay visitor can be a most helpful guide. Being a helpful guide requires some knowledge of the processes of grief. A variety of resources, some probably in your church's library, are available to give helpful information on the grief processes.

In ministry to the bereaved, it is important also that the visitor not minimize the feelings of grief and loss by too quick a recourse to the resurrection hope that we all have and share in Christ. The resurrection is not an automatic "cure" for death and grief. Nor is feeling sorrow and pain at the loss a denial of the resurrection hope. One can rest on the rock of resurrection hope even in tears. Research has shown that those bereaved persons who have been helped early to be aware of their grief, and to express it appropriately, have been more quickly healed of the trauma of death, than those who kept a stiff upper lip and avoided their grieving. Even in grief, it is possible to discover God as a refuge, our "portion in the land of the living" (Ps. 142:5).

A Patient's Bill of Rights

In 1972, the American Hospital Association developed a "patient's bill of rights" in the hope that "observance of these rights will contribute to more effective patient care and greater satisfaction for the patient, his physician, and the hospital organization." It is the expectation of the Association that these rights will be supported by the individual hospital on behalf of its patients. The Association also intends that these rights would not only sustain, but enhance the all important relationship between the physician and the patient.

These rights are affirmed by the American Hospital Association:

1. The patient has the right to considerate and respectful care.

2. The patient has the right to obtain from his physician complete current information concerning his diagnosis, treatment, and prognosis in terms the patient can be reasonably expected to understand.

When it is not medically advisable to give such information to the patient, the information should be made available to an appropriate person in his behalf. He has the right to know by name, the physician responsible for coordinating his care.

3. The patient has the right to receive from his physician information necessary to give informed consent prior to the start of any procedures and/or treatment. Except in emergencies, such information for informed consent, should include but not necessarily be limited to the specific procedure and/or treatment, the medically significant risks involved, and the probable duration of incapacitation. Where medically significant alternatives for care or treatment exist, or when the patient requests information concerning medical alternatives, the patient has the right to such information. The patient also has the right to know the name of the person responsible for the procedures and/or treatment.

4. The patient has the right to refuse treatment to the extent permitted by law, and to be informed of the medical consequences of his action.

5. The patient has the right to every consideration of his privacy concerning his own medical care program. Case discussion, consultation, examination, and treatment are confidential and should be conducted discreetly. Those not directly involved in his care must have the permission of the patient to be present.

6. The patient has the right to expect that all communications and records pertaining to his care should be treated as confidential.

7. The patient has the right to expect that within its capacity a hospital must make reasonable response to the request of a patient for services. The hospital must provide evaluation, service, and/or referral as indicated by the urgency of the case. When medically permissible, a patient may be transferred to another facility only after he has received complete information and explanation concerning the needs for and alternatives to such a transfer. The institution to which the patient is to be transferred must first have accepted the patient for transfer.

8. The patient has the right to obtain information as to any relationship of his hospital to other health care and educational institutions insofar as his care is concerned. The patient has the right to obtain information as to the existence of any professional relationships among individuals, by name, who are treating him.

9. The patient has the right to be advised if the hospital proposes to engage in or perform human experimentation affecting his care or treatment. The patient has the right to refuse to participate in such research projects.

10. The patient has the right to expect reasonable continuity of care. He has the right to know in advance what appointment times and physicians are available and where. The patient has the right to expect

that the hospital will provide a mechanism whereby he is informed by his physician or a delegate of the physician of the patient's continuing health care requirements following discharge.

11. The patient has the right to know what hospital rules and regulations apply to his conduct as a patient.

Common Medical Terms

The following list of prefixes and suffixes and common hospital abbreviations is intended as a helpful guide in your understanding the diagnostic terms you are likely to encounter in your hospital visiting. You may hear some medical terms used by the patient, by the doctor, or by nurses. You will find it helpful to become familiar with these terms in helping patients understand more clearly what the medical staff is speaking about. Be very careful, however, that you do not pretend to offer medical interpretations or medical advice. Avoid also using these technical terms in your conversations with medical staff or with the patients you are visiting unless they introduce them.

Prefixes

a	lack of (aseity, anemia)
anti	against, opposed to (antitoxin)
auto	self (auto-hypnosis)
bi	twice (bilateral hernia)

bio	life (biopsy)
brachial	arm, pertaining to the arm (brachial artery)
broncho	pertaining to bronchus (bronchitis)
cardi	pertaining to heart (cardiology)
derma	the skin (dermatitus)
ec, ex, ecto	out, outside (excise)
en, em	within, in
extra	outside
gastro	the stomach (gastritis)
haema, hema	the blood (hematology)
hemi	half (hemiplegia)
heter	different, opposite
hydro	water
hyper	excess (hyperacidity)
hypo	diminution as to degree (hypoglycemia)
hyster	womb (hysterectomy)
ileo	pertaining to the ileum (iliostomy)
infra	beneath, below
inter	between
intra	within
leuko	white (leukopenia)
macro	largeness, hypertrophy
mal	bad (malignant)
micro	smallness
mono	singleness
multi	number, many
myelo	referring to brain, spinal cord (osteomyelitis)
myo	pertaining to muscles
neo	new, recent, young (neonate)
nephro	referring to kidney (nephritis)
neuro	referring to nerve or neurology

ophthalmo	pertaining to eyes
ortho	straight, upright, correct
osteo	referring to bone (osteopath)
oto	referring to ear (otitis)
para	through, nearby
peri	about, around
poly	many, much (polyuria)
pseudo	false, spurious
pyo	pertaining to pus or purulency
retro	backward, behind
rhino	pertaining to nose (rhinitis)
semi	half, partly
super	above, in excess of

Suffixes

algia	pain in a part (neuralgia)
cele	a tumor, hernia, protrusion (hydrocele)
ectomy	excision, removal of (gastrectomy)
emia	denotes a condition of the blood
fuge	driving out, an expeller
graph	writing instrument, instrument
itis	inflammatory activity
lysis	separation into constituent parts
mania	mental affliction
meter	instrument for measuring
oma	tumor (glioma)
opia	pertaining to the eye (diplopia)
philia	to have an affinity for: (hemophilia)
phobia	morbid or exaggerated fear or dread (claustrophobia)
plasty	surgical plastic operation (rhinoplasty)
rrhagia	a hemorrhage or excessive discharge
rrhaphy	a stitching or suturing of a part
rrhea	an excessive discharge or secretion

scope | an instrument for making examination (stethoscope)
stomy | a suffix seen in the names of those operations in which an artificial opening is made (colostomy)
tomy | an incision
uria | pertaining to urine or urination
septic | poison or toxic substance
costal | ribs (intracostal—within the chest)

Common abbreviations used in hospitals

Dx | diagnosis
A.S.H. | arteriosclerotic heart
A.S.H.D. | arteriosclerotic heart disease
B.P., B/P | blood pressure
C.V.A. | cerebrovascular accident or "stroke"
C.A. | cancer
C.B.C. | complete blood count
E.K.G. | electrocardiogram
E.E.G. | electroencephalogram
I.V. | intravenous
N.P.O. | nothing by mouth
Rx | treatment
S.O.B. | short of breath
T.P.R. | temperature, pulse, respirations
b.i.d. | twice a day
t.i.d. | three times a day
g.i.d. | four times a day
g.d. | once a day
p.r.n. | whenever necessary

For Further Reading

Unfortunately, not a great deal has been written recently about ministry to the sick. That is one reason for this book. A number of the references cited here are out of print, but they are mentioned because they are classics in the field and are important for everyone who wishes to make a vocation of ministry to the sick. Out-of-print books may be found in church seminary libraries.

Becker, Ernest, *The Denial of Death*. New York: The Free Press, 1973.

Bittner, Vernon J., *Make Your Illness Count*. Minneapolis: Augsburg Publishing House, 1976.

A recently-written book by a Lutheran chaplain is directed toward those who are ill. It suggests that illness can be used as a resource in developing greater spiritual and emotional depth and maturity. It contains a number of helpful case illustrations. It is the kind of a book that a visitor to the sick might share with patients and discuss with them.

Bruder, Ernest E., *Ministering to Deeply Troubled People*. Englewood Cliffs: Prentice-Hall Inc., 1963. Out of print.

One of the few books available on ministry to people who are mentally or emotionally ill, it is a classic written by one of the pioneering professional mental hospital chaplains. While many of the concepts of mental illness have changed since this book was written, Chapter 3 contains valuable helps for visiting the mental hospital.

Cabot, Richard C. and Dicks, Russell L., *The Art of Ministering to the Sick*. New York: The Macmillan Company, 1936. Out of print.

This pioneering book in the field of modern pastoral care of the sick was written by one of the first 20th-century professional hospital chaplains in collaboration with a physician on the staff of Massachusetts General Hospital in Boston. Though written in the early 1920s, it still contains much valuable help in understanding illness and caring for the sick.

Cousins, Norman, *The Anatomy of an Illness As Perceived by the Patient*. New York: Bantam Books Inc., 1981.

Like Bittner's book, this one is intended especially for those who are sick. It is an account of Cousins' own battle with a life-threatening disease. The book suggests that emotional and spiritual attitudes can have much to do with the course of disease.

Dicks, Russell L., *You Came unto Me*. Durham: Duke University Department of Pastoral Care, 1951. Out of Print.

Written by the chaplain who wrote the classic *Art of Ministering to the Sick* for lay people, this book provides some helpful and concrete suggestions for lay ministry in the hospital.

Scherzer, Carl J., *Ministering to the Physically Ill*. Englewood Cliffs: Prentice-Hall Inc., 1963. Out of print.

Written by a professional hospital chaplain for pastoral use in enhancing ministry to the sick, this book contains helpful resources for understanding various types of illnesses and useful suggestions for scriptural resources, poetry, and prayers for use with the sick.

Westberg, Granger E., *Good Grief*. Philadelphia: Fortress, 1962.

Simply written, this book explains the process of grieving and how one can be helpful to oneself and others in living through the grieving process.

_____ , *Minister and Doctor Meet*. New York: Harper and Brothers, 1961. Out of print.

In this book Westberg is especially concerned about the functioning of the pastor or chaplain, the physician, and other members of the hospital professional staff as a health team. It contains some helpful chapters on understanding the perspective of the physician and on developing more effective communication between physician, pastor, and family. Westberg writes from a Lutheran theological point of view.

_____ , *Nurse, Pastor and Patient*. Rock Island: Augustana Book Concern, 1955. Out of print.

This book centers on more effective communication between nurse, pastor, and patient. Although written especially for nurses, it will be valuable also for lay visitors to the sick.